SAFARI LIVING

TANZANIA

Published in 2003 by:

Gallery Publications

P.O. Box 3181, Zanzibar

email: gallery@swahilicoast.com

London office:

32 Deanscroft Avenue

London NW9 8EN

email: zjafferji@aol.com

Photographs are available for commercial use from Impact Photos in the UK

e mail: library@impactphotos.demon.co.uk

Gemma Pitcher is available for copywriting assignments and can be contacted

by email: gemmapitcher@hotmail.com.

Graphic Designer: Antony Chunguli

Designed by Zanzibar Gallery Publishers

ISBN 9987 667 21 X

Dedicated to my parents, Abid and Bashira Jafferji.

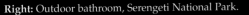

Right: Outdoor bathroom, Serengeti National Park.

SAFARI LIVING
TANZANIA

Photographs by Javed Jafferji
Written by Gemma Pitcher

Published by Gallery Publications

Contents

Left: Hand basin, Ruaha National Park.
Following page: Sunset at Greystoke Camp, Mahale Mountains National Park.

Introduction

For all its association with pith helmets and moustachioed Victorians, the safari existed in East Africa long before the coming of the white man. From the earliest times, caravans of porters carried oil, skins and rhinoceros horn out of the African interior to be traded with the seafaring people of the Swahili coast. These journeys - called in Arabic *safaris* - grew bigger and more complex with the rise of the slaving empire of Zanzibar. The scarlet flag of the Sultan of Zanzibar flew at the head of the vast caravans he sent out, proclaiming his dominions over an area so huge that none but a few of his servants would ever see it. The caravans wound their way inexorably in and out, from Zanzibar to Lake Victoria, escorting the slaves they had captured or leaving them dying by the roadside, their porters staggering under the great tusks of ivory or bundles of silks they carried.

Europeans, in their first explorations, changed little except the paraphernalia - their porters carried extra boxes of muskets and guns, or even cannon, for 'pacifying' villages and chiefdoms as they passed through, flanked by special regiments of guards recruited from Zanzibar before setting off. Zanzibar remained the jumping-off point for safaris to the mainland - the place where merchants must be haggled with, porters and guards engaged, officials called upon, safe passages secured and bribes paid. Nineteenth century Europeans who wished to set off into the wide, free spaces of the 'Dark Continent' had first to endure days, weeks, or even months of sweating, jostling and complaining in the stifling heat of Zanzibar's Stone Town.

The best known figure in this slow procession inward from Zanzibar was David Livingstone, the Scottish explorer and missionary who became so famously lost that Henry Morton Stanley was dispatched by the New York Times to find him. Livingstone spent his life searching for the one thing he never found - the source of the Nile River, the question of which engaged the hearts and minds of European society for decades.

The honour of 'settling the Nile question' finally went to the lesser-known John Hanning Speke, a hazy character eclipsed for the most part by his more famous travelling companion, Oriental linguist and explorer Richard Burton. It was Burton, in fact, who introduced the word 'safari' into the English vocabulary. But it was Speke who discovered Lake Victoria in 1858 and declared then and there: "The Nile is settled!" Travelling thousands of miles inland at the head of a huge train of porters, and sometimes so incapacitated by fever and illness that they had to be carried on litters, Burton and Speke managed to be the first Europeans to look upon both Lakes Tanganyika and Victoria. But fame came at a price -during the course of their safari, an insect crawled into

Left: The round, mosaic-lined swimming pool at Grumeti River Camp in the Western Serengeti.

Speke's ear and rendered him deaf, Burton was racked by fever and almost blind, and the two men were barely on speaking terms by the time they returned home in 1863.

The source of the mysterious 'fever' that racked every European explorer on safari and killed more than a few was the *anopheles* mosquito, not recognised as the source of malaria until 1898. The chills and cramps that the travellers complained of came from polluted water, which was not boiled before drinking until well into the twentieth century. Flannel underwear and thick tweed, accompanied by one or two felt hats and a thick, quilted spine pad, were considered the only appropriate dress for exploring south of the equator, where temperatures rose into the hundreds for weeks at a time. This terror of the sun lasted well into the twentieth century - as Elspeth Huxley reported: 'The sun was regarded as a kind of dangerous wild animal that would strike you down if you did not watch it every minute of the day between nine and four o'clock'. As for provisions, maize meal and meat shot along the way were the staples, supplemented with Fortnum and Mason delicacies eked out carefully until the last tin of *paté de foie gras* was gone.

Speke found it, but it was left to Henry Morton Stanley, another Victorian hero, to prove the source of the Nile. He also found time to locate the absent Dr Livingstone, tracking him to the banks of Lake Tanganyika at Ujiji after a journey lasting more than a year. Stanley was not a man to travel light - on his first safari, in 1871, he took over 400 porter loads of supplies, including in his retinue four porters who only carried brandy, wine and vinegar, and 22 who carried, in pieces, two boats, to be reassembled when a lake was reached. Finally came his huge bathtub, carried a thousand miles inland from the coast on the heads of two Africans. Nor was Stanley one to pass gently through a slice of untouched Africa - vigorous fighting at all times was the order of the day, and a trail of corpses and burnt villages was left in his wake to enhance his reputation as a man of action both at home and in his new-found domain.

Then as now, the image of a safari was everything. Headmen and porters' leaders wore special headdresses to identify themselves; drums were beaten, muskets fired and flutes played to announce the safari's arrival. Europeans, when marching into a village or a new chief's domain, wore full dress uniform, complete with swords, or in the case of early explorer Samuel Baker, full highland dress including a kilt and a Tam O'Shanter hat.

When night fell, porters built grass huts to sleep in at every stop; Europeans had canvas tents. Camp was broken before first light, and the shout of "*haya safari!*" announced the beginning of the day's trek, walking in the cool of the morning and stopping to rest during the heat of the day - the Europeans using the hot hours of inactivity for writing notes, bringing 'specimens' back to camp for examination, or studying compasses or theodolites.

The day of the European in East Africa was coming. By the end of the nineteenth century, the great slave caravans of the Sultan of Zanzibar were no more. Slavery had been abolished, the Sultan's power was at an end, and the safari caravans that set off into the interior were now mostly headed by white explorers, sportsmen or missionaries. As the colonial grip on East Africa tightened, British and German administrators took to the trails, forging paths for their governments until the whole map of East Africa was filled in and neatly demarcated. By 1914, over 90 per cent of Africa was claimed by Europeans.

It was at this point that the idea of the tourist was introduced into East Africa - as opposed to the gentleman explorers who confidently expected privation, threat, and hardship in return for the glory of a new 'discovery'. The bestsellers penned by the likes of Burton and Stanley had done their work, and the imagination of the moneyed public had been captured. A new breed of traveller had arrived; one who wanted to see, marvel (and shoot) at what had already been discovered - in comfort. The opening up of the Suez Canal made the East coast of Africa more accessible to the 'ordinary' adventurer, perhaps armed with one of the new-fangled cameras in addition to the usual battery of heavy guns.

A living transition between the old and new faces of the safari was Frederick Courtenay Selous, an old-time Victorian hero who made his name as an elephant hunter, explorer and naturalist. In 1909, however, he changed tack to pioneer the first and most famous of the leisure safaris of

Right: Hippo teeth adorn a writing table at Selous Safari Camp.

the new era. President Theodore Roosevelt of the United States, enervated by years of confinement in the White House, chose an African safari over a third term of presidency, and Selous was his 'white hunter' - a term that eventually became a common cipher for all that the modern age considered brave, manly and resourceful. The Roosevelt safari effectively began the East African tourist industry, launching hundreds of wealthy American would-be adventurers in the wake of their former leader.

When the First World War broke out in 1914, Selous transformed his bush skills and deadly shooting ability into military prowess. He took command of a ragged group known as the 'Legion of Frontiersmen', a special African unit including a lighthouse keeper, several acrobats and a couple of Texas cowboys. After leading patrols of exhausted men forty years his junior through heavy swamps for hours on end, Selous would take off in the evening with a butterfly net to collect specimens. He fell at last near Beho Beho in the modern-day Selous Game Reserve, shot by a German sniper whose officer later made a formal apology to the British command.

After the First World War the former German East Africa became Tanganyika - a word meaning 'the bush beyond Tanga' - held on a special United Nations mandate by Britain. As the country became anglicized, the safari industry enjoyed a boom. Arusha was the focal point of Tanganyika's safaris, built as it was in between the newly 'discovered' wonderlands of the Serengeti and the Ngorongoro Crater. It was secondary to Nairobi, but as Nairobi's old guard pioneers and settlers were gradually replaced by a less adventurous, more dissolute type of settler - exemplified by the antics of the Happy Valley set - Tanganyika evolved into a centre for the tougher and more serious type of European safarigoer.

The coming of the motor car to East Africa between the wars changed the face of safari forever, many thought for the worse. Where once trains of porters had set out, convoys of vehicles instead bumped their way into the wilderness, and patient stalks on foot were at times replaced by dragging meat behind vehicles and shooting lions from inside the car - a practice widely condemned by the old guard. Later, tiny planes buzzed clients between camps, helped hunters by spotting the best elephant from the air, or were sent up daily to fetch the newspaper from Arusha to the Serengeti.

As safaris became more accessible, they also became more fashionable, and the idea of an adventure in the African wilderness was heightened in the public consciousness by the Hollywood movies of the 1920s and 30s. When American writer Ernest Hemingway arrived in East Africa, safari found a new popular medium - literature. A journey to the African wilderness became not only adventurous, but glamorous - fame and money were the new gods of the modern age, and they adopted the safari as their own.

When the future Edward VIII of England came out to Tanganyika on safari in 1928, however, he surprised his white hunters Denys Finch Hatton and Bror Blixen by eschewing many of the expected comforts and accessories of the day. The then Prince of Wales was described by Blixen as "one of the three or four toughest sportsmen I have been out with, or perhaps the toughest of them all". He thought nothing of stalking elephant on foot for several days in a row, marching through blistering heat and sleeping in a simple tent on the ground.

But for most clients, the trappings were all. Double walled tents, mosquito netting, chemical toilets, air mattresses and mess tables were *de rigueur*. Each day had a strict routine - breakfast in the dark, hunting or game-watching in the early morning, back to camp for lunch and afternoon rest; out again until dark, then a hot bath, cocktails and dinner in pyjamas and thigh-high mosquito-boots. Anything at all could be brought on safari if the clients were willing to pay - African veteran JA Hunter remembered a safari that included a private armoured car, a mobile cinema, several motorcycle messengers, a generating plant, a medical lorry (complete with x-ray machine), and a mobile drawing room with a grand piano.

The Second World War put paid to these kinds of antics, at least for a few years. Once again the white hunters swapped animal targets for human ones - most went north to Abyssinia to fight the Italians. When the smoke cleared, and the 1950s began, another phenomenon had appeared that was to change the face of the safari yet again - mass air travel. Big four-engined aircraft, the next generation of World War Two bombers, began to land at Nairobi airport. From here it was only a few hours drive to Tanganyika's northern 'game protected areas', which were given an added allure as the Mau Mau crisis - an African uprising - terrorised Kenya from

Left: A fly-camp bathroom at Sand Rivers in the Selous Game Reserve - hot water in a canvas bucket shower and a bar of finest soap perched on a hippo skull.

1953. But there were plenty of tourists to go round - the mass air travel revolution and post-war economic expansion meant that safari travel had become accessible to the middle classes as well as to the super-rich.

As the number of safari hunters grew, pressures on the most popular trophy animals became intolerable - their numbers, already in decline, were reaching crisis levels. Even with the decline of hunting in favour of the less expensive photographic or game-watching safaris, steps were needed to preserve both habitat and the animals themselves. The response of the colonial administration was the creation of 'Game Reserves', areas where game and environment were specially protected and which went on - after a considerable struggle on the part of the conservationists of the day - to become the post-independence National Parks. By the end of the 1950s, the transition from hunting as the primary safari activity was complete. Most visitors to East Africa from the 1960s onwards came to watch game in protected areas, not to wander at will in search of quarry to shoot.

The first permanent structures for the new breed of lower-budget safari visitors were the resthouses erected by the colonial government in the 1950s. Such simple buildings, which usually comprised just a bedroom and a kitchen area, were intended for use by travelling government officials, but available at other times for visitors. In the 1960s, these resthouses evolved into the early safari lodges, precursors of those in use today. Safari accommodation - both private and public - has been evolving ever since, proliferating into areas of wilderness once only accessible to the hardiest caravan of porters, and finding form in anything from a tented village to a baroque palace. The mobile cinemas and grand pianos of the 1930s have been replaced by the satellite phones, internet servers and jacuzzis of the 21st century.

One thing, though, will never change. Today's safarigoers, for all the luxury and sophistication with which they are surrounded, are still searching for the same experience sought by Stanley and Livingstone two centuries ago - a closeness to the wild earth, a sense of the smallness of humanity upon the planet, and an understanding of a place and a culture alien to their own. The truth, for the lucky few that discover it, is that none of the trappings really matter. In the words of American naturalist John Muir: "Only by going alone in silence, without baggage, can one truly get into the heart of the wilderness. All other travel is mere dust and hotels and chatter."

Right: The straw pavilions at Mwagusi Safari Camp blend in perfectly with the bush that surrounds them.

Ngorongoro Crater

The Ngorongoro Crater more properly described as a caldera - actually the largest perfect collapsed volcanic caldera in the world. Calderas are created when the inside of an active volcano sinks during a period of inactivity, leaving a vast hole inside the mountain. As the hole increases, the mountain eventually becomes unstable and the upper cone of the volcano collapses. The peak of the Ngorongoro volcano is thought to have been even higher than Kilimanjaro before it collapsed some 2.5 million years ago.

One hundred square miles in area, and with an average wall height of 600 metres, the Ngorongoro Crater floor forms a microcosm of African habitats, with grassland, swamps, lakes, rivers and forest all spread out over a relatively small area. The animal and bird species are as diverse as the landscape – bachelor herds of huge elephants roam the crater floor, browsing knee-deep in the yellow *beitens* flowers that carpet the area every spring; they ascend only when a signal, inaudible to human ears, tells them one of the females who live on the rim of the crater is in oestrus. Lion, so accustomed to game-viewing vehicles that they barely raise their heads at an approaching engine, laze in the marshy grass of the Mandusi Swamp. In the Lerai forest, troops of baboon chatter angrily at the lazy form of a leopard stretched along a yellow-bark acacia branch. Flocks of delicately coloured flamingos, heads between feet, dabble in the salty waters of Lake Magadi. The crater floor has been described as 'a living Ark' – hundreds of species coexisting in harmony in a setting of outstanding natural beauty.

But Ngorongoro – encompassing both the crater itself and the surrounding three thousand square miles of dense rainforest, volcanic highlands and rolling plains – is not a national park, but a conservation area, acting not only as a nature reserve, but as an eco-system whose protection and management includes the welfare of the people who consider it to be their traditional homeland. The Maasai are partners in the management of the area, driving their cattle to the crater floor for water and salt during the day, and returning to their traditional homesteads in the surrounding area during the night.

Left: One of the Crater's magnificent bull elephants, knee deep in a sea of yellow *beitens* flowers.

Ngorongoro Crater Lodge
Chandeliers in a mud hut

Often described, inaccurately, as the 'Maasai Versailles', Ngorongoro Crater Lodge is that rare thing – a truly original hotel. The brainchild of South African architects Silvio and Lesley Rech, and interior designer Chris Browne, the 'Crater Lodge' as it is affectionately known, is a once seen, never forgotten masterpiece of design. Many of the hotel's guests even find it difficult to tear themselves away from the experience of staying at the Lodge in order to descend to the floor of the Ngorongoro Crater, one of the most richly rewarding game-viewing areas in Africa…

'Maasai Versailles' isn't quite right as a description, firstly because the simple mud huts of the exterior are nothing like Maasai dwellings, but in fact owe more in inspiration to the houses or fortresses of West Africa. Tall mud-brick chimneys and abstract wall designs apart, the relative simplicity of the Lodge's exterior structures gives little hint of its flamboyant interior.

Stepping through the doors of Crater Lodge, the visitor is greeted not by the formality of a French palace, but rather by a tongue-in-cheek operatic fantasy, filtered through the sensibilities of a grand English country house. Elegantly upholstered sofas contrast with extravagant Art Deco sculptures, and glittering chandeliers hang from the woven banana-leaf roof. The design scheme of Crater Lodge is based on the idea that the early settlers in Tanzania lived in simple, earth dwellings like their African neighbours, but went to huge trouble to import the home comforts and decorations of their European roots. This incongruity – 'the unpacking of the trunks' - lies at the heart of Crater Lodge's interior design, which mixes artefacts and furnishings from Europe with souvenirs collected from Tanzania's Arab-influenced coast.

The keynote at Crater Lodge is drama. From the impossibly grand, firelit dining areas to the enormous, velvet-draped beds, the lodge responds to the volcanic moods of the Ngorongoro Crater itself, a vast amphitheatre in view from every window and fascinating in its constantly changing patterns of light and shade, burning sunlight and boiling cloud. The genius of Crater Lodge lies in treading the fine line between kitsch and tastelessness and extravagance and wit. Anywhere else in Africa, a hotel this outrageous would seem out of place, but perched as it is on the lip of one of the most dramatic natural wonders of the world, such a fantastical structure seems entirely appropriate. Where else in the world can guests have an aromatherapy massage in front of a roaring fire while gazing down into a volcanic crater, one of the earth's most breathtaking natural spectacles?

Romance is the other major factor at Crater Lodge – the bedrooms are enormous, baroque, almost camp in their homage to the passionate traditions of the Paris Opera. Silk-upholstered footstools stand next to claw-footed bathtubs scattered with rose petals, taffeta curtains and gilt-framed mirrors glinting in the candlelight.

South Camp and Main Camp, side by side on the crest of a hill, are spectacular enough, but the glass-fronted Tree Camp, a private, more secluded collection of just six bedrooms hidden from the rest of the Lodge by lush vegetation, is the most exquisite of all. Viewed through the glass walls of the Tree Camp dining room, the crater seems closer and more immediate, the mists that cover the rim in the mornings melting away by lunchtime to reveal the shadows of clouds chasing each other across the vast green expanse of the caldera floor.

Left: The mess area of Tree Camp at Ngorongoro - an eclectic space enclosed by glass and looking out over the crater floor.

Above: A pewter ice bucket and tongs - one of many decadent, 1920s-style touches that characterise the Lodge's design.
Right: The bathrooms are as large as the bedrooms and positively operatic with their freestanding claw baths, gold taffeta curtains and gilt-edged mirrors.

Above: Bucks fizz on a rose-strewn tray awaits new arrivals at the Crater Lodge.
Right: A myriad of eccentric and eclectic details - some African, some European, some new, some antique - make up the Lodge's unforgettable style.

Left: The rich red upholstery of Tree Camp's outside dining terrace contrasts with the blue highland sky and the constantly changing pattern of colours on the crater floor far below.

Above: The outside of the Crater Lodge is built to resemble a West African village, with muted, muddy colours in sharp contrast to the vibrant interior design.

Left: The Lodge's palatial dining room, with firelight glinting on the sparkling white table linen and silver cutlery.

Above: The sitting rooms at the Crater Lodge resemble the interior of an old fashioned English country house with their open fireplaces, upholstered armchairs and rich, warm fabrics.

 # The Maasai

"Their style is not an assumed manner, nor an imitation of a foreign perfection; it has grown from the inside, and is an expression of the race and its history, and their weapons and finery are as much a part of their being as are a stag's antlers."

Karen Blixen, *Out of Africa*

Often associated solely with Kenya, Maasailand actually spans the Tanzania/Kenya border. The Maasai are undoubtedly one of the most instantly recognised ethnic groups in Africa, and their unique and fiercely guarded pastoralist culture has survived robustly into the 21st century.

Unlike, for example, the Makonde woodcarvers in the south of Tanzania, the art of the Maasai is principally one of decoration rather than monumental sculpture, particularly body adornment to signify age or marital status. Beads are the most distinctive element to be found in personal clothing or jewellery, with considerable artistic talent manifested in the way beads are used for embellishment, often in conjunction with expertly worked leather.

Maasai women wear elaborate ensembles of beaded clothing and adornment, including necklaces and ear ornaments, to assert their position within their own society. Ear ornaments or clothing consist of beads sewn onto a softened cow hide backing, arranged in such a way as to create balanced patterns of strong colours such as white, red, and green. Colour schemes in beadwork design began with the primary colours of the bead materials available to the Maasai before the advent of Europeans - white from clay, bone or shells, black or blue from iron or charcoal, and red from seeds, ivory or copper. The arrival of European glass trade beads increased the colour spectrum of Maasai beadwork, with modern glass beads replacing older, more organic materials. This type of Maasai art is included in the design schemes of modern interior spaces all over Tanzania.

Left above: Maasai beadwork and *shukas*, or blankets, on display at Grumeti River Camp.
Below: Maasai women herd donkeys in the Ngorongoro Highlands.
Right: Maasai neck collars.

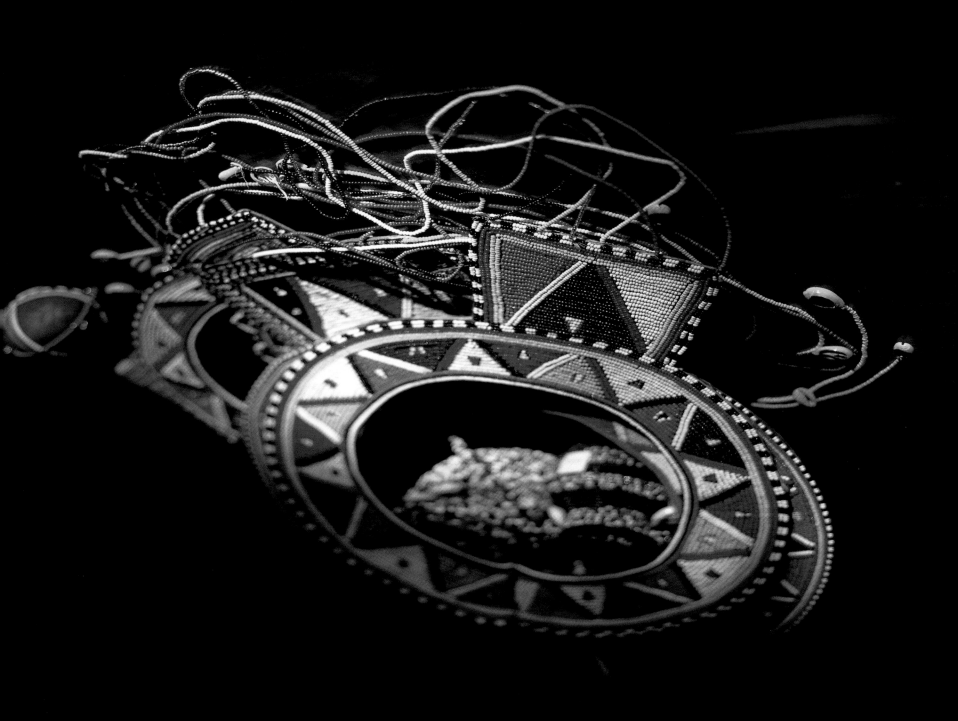

Serengeti National Park

Siringitu in Maasai - "the place where the land moves on forever". Home of mankind's first footprints and the spectacle of the great migration. One of the oldest ecosystems on earth. Waving golden grasses, flat-topped acacia trees, distant blue hills. Giraffes, lions, cheetah. How do you write about the Serengeti without using up every cliché in the Travel Writer's Handbook?

Perhaps in the words of Alan Moorehead, in the introduction to the famous book *Serengeti Shall Not Die*: "Anyone who can go to the Serengeti, and does not, is mad." Certainly, for the first time visitor to East Africa, a visit to the Serengeti will guarantee immersion in that quintessential African landscape immortalised in a million films, album covers and cheap aftershave advertisements.

But stay longer, come back again, and you'll get to know the Serengeti the chocolate boxes have missed. The dry, blackened hills of the Lobo region, studded with granite outcrops and burnt by a thousand grass fires. The sulphurous, muddied waters of a dam churned to midden by the frantic hooves of a million migrating wildebeest. A vulture perched in a dead tree, stark against a pale-blue sky, contemplating the flat, featureless short-grass plains of the long dry season. These are the harsher, less easily 'ticked off' aspects of Africa's most famous national park, but for the visitor with time enough to experience the full scope of the Serengeti, sights like these are none the less beautiful.

One thing is for certain – whether visiting the Serengeti for days, weeks or months, modern Tanzania has provided today's travellers with a wealth of cutting-edge, luxurious and innovatively designed lodges and camps, all forming entirely different yet uniformly satisfying bases from which to explore the most famous wildlife area in the world.

Left: Dust, flies, milling confusion and sudden eddying panic - thousands of wildebeest and zebra congregate around a tributary of the Seronera River in preparation for another leg of their annual migration.

Grumeti River Camp

Fantasy in the western corridor

"Our camp was cuddled in the crook of a low mountain's arm, but behind was plain, a brilliant yellow plain dotted with blue-and-white flowers. Wherever you looked there was life. Five thousand wildebeest there. Five thousand zebras yonder. A herd of buffalo on the river. If you grew grass on Times Square and cleaned up the air and made it suddenly quiet and filled it with animals instead of people, you might approach some likely approximation of what I saw that morning, with the blue sky and the hills green and the plain yellow and blue and white."

So wrote American hunter Robert Ruark of his 1940s 'paradise' camp on the banks of the Grumeti River. Half a century on, the Serengeti's western corridor, with its combination of plains, riverine forest and thorn scrub, remains one of the most fascinating locations in the world to watch wildlife. The main event happens every dry season, when the annual wildebeest migration crosses the Grumeti River on its way north – thousands upon thousands of desperately lowing herbivores plunging over the banks and into the water, with as many deaths occurring from simple drowning as from the famous onslaught of the river's notorious giant crocodiles. But Grumeti Camp is also fortunate to be surrounded by a permanent population of zebra, antelope and wildebeest, who enjoy the region's non-stop water supply and keep a healthy population of lion, cheetah and leopard well fed, ensuring excellent game viewing all year round.

But for all its beauty, the landscape of this region is harsh and unforgiving, with endless tawny-brown grasses stretching out towards the smoke of grass fires on the horizon under a dry, pitiless sun. After several hours hard driving over the arid plains, arriving at Grumeti River Camp feels rather like coming to an oasis in the middle of the desert – set next to a tranquil backwater of the river, the camp exudes a cool, green serenity echoed by the placidly honking hippos in the pool next to the breakfast lawn.

Water and sun – the two essentials of life in the Serengeti - are the major themes in the décor of the camp. The round plunge pool, a welcome respite from the heat of the day, is adorned with a mosaic sun motif, and the colours chosen for the upholstery of the lounge and dining room are fiery oranges and yellows. The exterior structures of the camp are muted, with the subtle red clay and thatch walls and roofs contrasting with a funky, vibrant interior based around the beadwork and textiles of West African design traditions. Contemporary pieces of chunky glassware in cool watery greens and blues, together with eccentrically shaped cast iron sculptures, finish off the ultra-modern look of the public spaces.

The bedrooms continue the fun, irreverent feel of the rest of the camp, with canvas-fronted tents backed onto permanently structured bathrooms. Innovative outside showers allow guests to look up at the stars through a cast iron astronomical dome while washing off the dust of the day. Bedspreads are made from the same colourful *kente* style cloth as the rugs scattered over the smooth cement floor, and above the pillows rises an enormous, exuberant wooden bedhead, shaped like the crown of a fairytale monarch.

Left: Grumeti River Camp's communal spaces are open to the air and furnished with contemporary cast-iron and glass tables, West African beaded figures and enormous crocodile skulls salvaged from the nearby river.

Above: An eccentric beaded figure from West Africa, one of the many offbeat touches at Grumeti River Camp.
Right: Vibrant neon greens, oranges and blues compete with pink cement walls and green glass chandeliers in Grumeti's lounge area.

Left: Each of Grumeti's vast tents has a private stone verandah outside, smooth cement floors decorated with glass mosaics, and is furnished with easy chairs and floor cushions.

Above: A bed at Grumeti River Camp - fit for a fairytale monarch.

Above and right: Beading, glasswork, mosaic and natural elements such as earthenware are combined to fuse nature with artiface in Grumeti's bold design scheme.

Kirawira Luxury Tented Camp
Edwardian elegance

Myles Turner, pioneering park warden of the Serengeti in the 1950s and 60s, describes Kirawira in his memoirs as one of the most beautiful campsites in the park, a wonderful spot in the western corridor surrounded by 'miles of open, tawny country broken with sanseveria thickets and covered with zebra, wildebeest, eland, gazelle and buffalo'.

Turner, however, makes no mention of the story related by another conservationist, Alistair Graham, in his book *Eyelids of the Morning*, a study of the Nile crocodile. According to Graham, Kirawira takes its name from a certain notorious poacher named Kwehahura, who defied the efforts of Turner and his park rangers to capture him for many years. Surprised one day by a patrol, he took off at a run for the bush along the nearby Grumeti river. Once there, he leapt without hesitation into a deep pool, hoping to swim across and evade his followers. The splash of Kwehahura entering the water was followed seconds later by that of another, heavier, body, and by the time the rangers arrived at the riverbank nothing was left of the poacher but a few swirls of muddy water. The spot is named Kirawira in his honour.

Today, however, the name Kirawira has other, happier associations. Kirawira Luxury Tented Camp has gained a well-earned reputation as a camp where the old-fashioned gentleman (and lady) explorers of past centuries would not feel out of place. Kirawira is determinedly nostalgic in feel, with a definite emphasis on the finer things in life. The walls at Kirawira may be made of canvas, but the interior spaces are furnished in grand style, with no concession to the camp's wild and remote location. Edwardian elegance is everywhere, from the straight-backed chairs of the sitting room to the fine blue-and-white china and damask tablecloths of the dining tent.

Kirawira's bedroom tents look out across a stunning vista of dark-green plains, distant blue-green hills and wheeling birds of prey. Inside, pretty patchwork quilts and lace mosquito nets emphasise the vintage feel of the rooms, and vast bathrooms with black and white tiles and marble sinks are lit by old-fashioned brass lamps.

In the heat of the day, Kirawira's guests are found around the camp's magnificent lagoon swimming area, built into the side of the hill. Water cascades through shady, whispering bush to a series of two tiled pools, linked by a waterfall. Green canvas umbrellas and sun beds are arranged on an elegant slatted deck that looks out across the plains.

Dining at Kirawira is formal, with champagne for breakfast and five courses at dinner and lunch, all served by lamplight in the dining tent. After dinner, the softly-lit art deco private bar, decanters of port and sherry ready alongside the finest cigars, gleams temptingly, and leather upholstered armchairs beckon guests for a nightcap taken listening to the gentle sounds of the African night outside.

Left: An ornate Art Deco style bar is the centrepiece of Kirawira's period drawing room.

Left and above: Antiques such as an old-fashioned gramophone and a brass *samavat*, or water container, add interesting touches to the sitting areas at Kirawira.

Klein's Camp

A frontiersman's dream in the rugged north

The dramatic, craggy scenery of the Kuka Hills in the northern Serengeti was once the scene of desperate battles between the local Maasai and their Kurya neighbours, who descended from Kenya – just the other side of the pass – on cattle raids. Today these bright green, fertile hills are more of a peaceful refuge than a battleground, with the Maasai villagers who still inhabit this private concession leasing their hereditary land for game viewing by guests at the exclusive Klein's Camp.

Klein's Camp, cresting the spine of the Kuka Hills and looking down over the valleys that run to the Maasai Mara, is named after Al Klein, an American white hunter who brought his safari clients to the area in search of its legendary big game, and later established a vegetable garden for the use of fellow safari outfitters on a plot close to the site of the present day camp. Today, the area is still known as a farm, rather than a reserve, with the Maasai villagers providing the camp with vegetables and honey from their *shambas*, or agricultural plots.

'Camp' is in fact rather a misleading term, as the structures of Klein's Camp are made from local stone rather than canvas. But despite its permanent nature, Klein's retains every bit of the pioneering atmosphere of the old days, with just ten frontier-style cottages perched on a high ridge, and a convivial, hard-drinking bar that commands an 180 degree view of the surrounding countryside. Anqtique safari paraphernalia is everywhere – a leather-covered game of backgammon, a 1920s compass, a mahogany cigar case. Klein's has a truly authentic, unpretentious feel to it, with no sense that the robust atmosphere has been manufactured or contrived.

The colours and décor at Klein's are masculine and muted – leather, animal prints, creams and browns – but the light and airy cottage interiors have the cheerful, wholesome feel of an Edwardian farmhouse, with thousands of miles of Africa receding from the edge of their enormous double beds, covered with striped cotton eiderdowns and soft amber blankets. Each cottage has a private flagstone terrace furnished with canvas safari chairs - perfect for sipping a leisurely sundowner while scanning the plains below for elephant, buffalo or giraffe.

Situated as it is on private land rather than within the Serengeti National Park, Klein's Camp is in the fortunate position of being able to take guests on game drives after dark. Many animals – especially large predators such as lion and leopard – are more active during the hours of darkness, and driving around at night, armed with a powerful tungsten lamp and guided by an expert Maasai tracker, is far more exciting than game viewing in the daytime. With no set game drive times, wildlife watchers are free to stay out all night if they so wish, returning to the camp in the small hours for a nightcap before bed!

Another privilege of being allowed to drive at night is so-called 'bush banqueting' – a slap-up dinner served a few kilometres from the camp in the heart of the wilderness, with dining tables, a barbeque, and of course a magnificent bar, all set up in full formal style in a clearing lit only by hurricane lamps and a blazing fire. As the meal draws to a close, the distant roaring of lions can be heard from the surrounding bush - and the real adventure begins as guests pile into Land Rovers and set off in pursuit…

Left: The rich browns and oranges of the Klein's Camp mess area are backed by the green tapestry of the Kuka hills outside.

Left and above: The flagstone terraces outside each room have canvas chairs for sundowners, scanning the vast blue-green expanse of hills opposite for game or just birdwatching in the bushes on the nearest slope.

Above and right: Klein's masculine, unpretentious bar area holds interesting safari antiques, old board games, and original pieces of Maasai bead and leather work alongside an impressive array of bottles!

Left and above: The curve of the walls in the mess area at Klein's is echoed by an enormous circular fireplace, protected by a vast cast-iron hood.

Kusini Camp

Green canvas among the kopjes

Often described as 'islands' in a sea of grass, the huge granite outcrops known as kopjes (pronounced 'copies') are an essential feature of the Serengeti. Rising like castles from the yellow sea of the surrounding prairies, kopjes are a reminder of the region's volcanic past. These vast, jumbled boulders are sanctuaries for predators such as spotted hyena and lion, as well as prey species such as rock hyrax and nimble klipspringer antelope. One of the greatest pleasures in the Serengeti is to climb the warm, lichen-stained stone of a kopje and settle down to watch sunrise or sunset spread out across the plains below.

The monumental *Hambi ya Mwaki Nyeb* kopjes are the centrepiece of Kusini Camp, a traditional, no-nonsense East African style affair of green canvas tents and hurricane lamps set among the vast open spaces of the Serengeti's southern short-grass plains. The dining/sitting room – or mess as it is known here – is a long, low tent with a stained cypress-wood floor, dwarfed by the enormous mass of rock behind it. The interior is simply furnished with Zanzibari carved furniture and colourful rugs, and a huge awning outside gives welcome shade in the heat of the day. A handsome wood sideboard at the end of the dining room is decorated with arrangements of dried Serengeti grasses, guinea fowl feathers and porcupine quills. At sundowner time, cushions and a mobile bar are carried to the top of the nearest kopje, and guests sip ice-cold Safari lager as the sky turns pink and the sun disappears rapidly below the distant horizon.

Kusini Camp is 40 kilometres in any direction from the nearest habitation – one can stand on the top of the kopje and turn slowly through 360 degrees without seeing a sign of modern civilisation or even human life. This feeling of remoteness and wilderness is key to the appeal of the camp, where elephant and buffalo browse between the tents at night, and a rare striped hyena ventures in from the evening darkness to lie and listen to the tall tales being told around the campfire. Game viewing here is an all-day activity, with Land Rovers bumping across the plains in search of cheetah (which have even been known to clamber onto the bonnets of cars in search of a lookout point!), lion and, in the wet season, the vast migratory herds of wildebeest that visit the southern grasslands each year.

The nine bedroom tents are positioned far enough from each other to ensure a feeling of utter privacy and seclusion – a far cry from the rows of interconnecting guy ropes at some other safari camps. Each is set on a wooden deck, with a classic Edwardian-style interior conceived by the British firm Designers' Guild. Egyptian cotton sheets, leather luggage racks and brass art deco lamps prove that living in the bush needn't be basic or uncomfortable – the porcelain sink, old fashioned taps and thick cotton towels of the bathroom – not to mention an impressive array of Molton Brown toiletries – provide unabashed luxury fit for one of the grand hunting safaris of Tanzania's past.

Left: Sunset drinks perched on top of Kusini's spectacular kopje.

Above: Kusini's tent interiors were created by London's Designers Guild, with brightly checked blankets and art-deco style brass lamps. Hot water bottles are covered with Maasai blanket material.

Right: Kusini's library features a full astonomical telescope, an impressive collection of wildlife books and comfortable chintz sofas.

Migration Camp

T h u n d e r i n g   h o o v e s   b e t w e e n   t h e   g u y   r o p e s

The famous annual migration of wildebeest, zebra and other grazing herbivores in the Serengeti - and its neighbour the Maasai Mara in Kenya - is often thought of as one single, intense and short-lived event. In fact, the migration is a vast circle of constant movement, travelling all year round through the seasons of rain and drought that make up the Serengeti's annual weather cycle. Enormous herds of up to two million animals move in seemingly endless columns between the dryer southern plains of the Serengeti-Mara ecosystem and the moist northern woodlands, then back again, grazing, mating and giving birth on the way. The grunting, dusty mass of the migration is trailed by a variety of predators and scavengers, with lion, hyena and vultures all waiting to fall upon weakened individuals or those that fall behind. The phenomenon of the Serengeti migration is one of the last mass movements of animals still taking place on earth, and undoubtedly one of the greatest wonders of the natural world.

Migration Camp, set amidst the craggy, dramatic scenery of the northern Serengeti, is positioned squarely in the path of the main bulk of the migration as, prompted by the beginning of the dry season, the herds stream north and west towards the Maasai Mara. During the migration season, July to September, guests in the camp are frequently woken at night by the sound of thundering hooves and emerge onto their private verandahs to watch the frantic wildebeest race between the tents in the moonlight, lowing mournfully.

The hilltop on which the camp now sits is known as Poachers' Lookout, and was formerly a popular spot for the Serengeti rangers to spy out the telltale threads of smoke that signalled the fires of illegal hunters and trappers. Maximum attention has been given to fitting the camp around the existing natural features of the surrounding area. Steps have been discreetly cut into the hillside, leading to a timbered and cantilevered bar, library and dining terrace - even the acacia and fig trees that grow through the eucalyptus wood deck have been left untouched. From the bar and library, panoramic views across the surrounding boulders and woodlands are accompanied by the unseen grunting of hippos, just out of sight among the trees of the river bed below. A kidney shaped swimming pool is the only splash of colour among the muted greens, creams and browns.

The terrain around Migration Camp, with its many trees, tumbled boulders and plentiful hiding spots, makes it an excellent base from which to search out leopard, the hardest to find of all the big cats. In and around the camp, eagles and vultures nest in the cliffs above the river, lizards skitter across the sun deck, and hyraxes scamper down from the rocks to peer inquisitively into the bar.

The bedrooms at Migration are traditional East African safari tents, some raised on stilts for a better view of the wooded slopes leading down to the Grumeti River just below. The honeymoon suite, set high above the rest of the camp under a huge, gnarled fig tree, has a sunken bath in the wooden deck behind it, allowing for an open-air sunset wallow among the rocky crevices of the hillside, as eagles wheel on the air currents above.

Left: The decadent sunken bath, set into the rocky hillside behind Migration Camp's honeymoon suite.

Above and right: The eucalyptus wood pool deck at Migration Camp is built around several fig and acacia trees, which grow up through the sun-warmed planks.

Left: Migration camp is built to face the spectacular Serengeti sunsets.
Above: Wildebeest that didn't survive the annual migration find a new destiny as lamps dotted around the dining area...

Above: Evening light gleams on the long wooden bar.
Right: Migration's handsome library is furnished in colonial style with heavy wood tables and wicker basket chairs.

Ballooning

A balloon safari in the Serengeti National Park starts with a bleary-eyed pre-dawn drive through the darkness of the bush to the departure point. Still in darkness, the whoosh and flare of the balloon's burners are shockingly dramatic, orange against the blackness, as the giant globe of the balloon slowly inflates and rises off the ground. Once afloat, one clambers into the wicker basket secured to the bonnet of a pickup truck, the ropes are freed, and with another deafening blast from the burners the balloon surges upwards.

The powerful burners have to be ignited every few minutes to keep the 100 foot balloon filled with heat. But in between their roars, the silence is absolute - freed from the dust and hurry of life at ground level, the balloon floats serenely on air currents, skimming just overhead unnoticed by pools of honking hippos, and almost touching the migrating wildebeest plodding in endless lines across the plains. Several more burner blasts, and the balloon can lift to 1000 feet, changing the perspective of the landscape so that purple hills in the far distance, gilded by the emerging sun, become visible, details blur and change and the full vastness of the Serengeti's 'endless plains' becomes apparent.

The balloon comes bumping to earth as the sun begins to warm the air in earnest, frequently touching down among herds of grazing antelope or zebra, so used to the sight of this strange beast that they barely raise their heads from the grass at its arrival. A decadent breakfast is laid out on a trestle table under a nearby tree - sizzling bacon and sausages on a barbeque, soft croissants wrapped in napkins, champagne in crystal glasses and succulent fruit set on dazzling white china. The experience is pure *Out of Africa*, sheer indulgence in the midst of the wilderness.

Left and right: Balloons in preparation and in flight over the Serengeti.

Tarangire National Park

During Tarangire's dry season, day after day of cloudless skies seem to suck all moisture from the landscape, turning the waving grasses to platinum blonde, brittle as straw. The plains for miles around, inside and outside the park, are dry and parched, with the only source of water being the Tarangire River, shallow and brackish yet providing the lifeblood of the park and the means of survival for a huge population of herbivores and their attendant predators.

Herds of elephant three hundred strong dig in the damp earth of the riverbed in search of underground springs, while wildebeest, zebra, buffalo, and gazelle mingle with rarer species such as eland and oryx around each shrinking lagoon. Python climb into the shade of the trees that line Tarangire's massive southern swamps and hang there, like giant malignant fruit, coils neatly arranged over the branches in a perfect sphere. Leopard and lion also ascend the trees, limbs loose and comfortable and tails twitching in the heat of the day, awaiting the coming of night and their imminent feast of impala, buffalo or hartebeest. Tarangire is home to enormous troops of baboon, insolently swaggering along the centre of the road or barking in alarm from the treetops at the approach of a predator, with tiny babies clutching their mother's stomachs, round-eyed and wondering.

In the wet season, wildlife populations scatter across the surrounding plains of the Maasai steppe, but the park's own beauty comes to life in verdant green pastures, lush swamps and carpets of sparkling wild flowers, reflecting the watery blue of the sky. Tarangire's endless variety of birds – the most breeding species in one habitat anywhere in the world - include plovers, larks, bustard and grouse, found wading in the swamps, perched on small bushes or pacing the dryer ground, sharp eyes alert for danger.

Tarangire's huge herds of elephant rival the park's monstrous baobab trees as its most celebrated feature – ancient matriarchs, feisty young bulls and tiny, stumbling calves are ever present to fascinate visitors with their grace, intelligence and power. Elephant populations are particularly dense during the dry season in the park's easily accessible northern reaches, with herds of cows with calves and massive, solitary bulls pacing casually across the roads in search of grazing, shade or water.

Tarangire's vast wilderness zone, a part of the park many casual visitors never even dream exists, is a paradise for walking safaris, the only form of tourism allowed in this precious southern region. Visitors can explore the rivers, swamps and plains of this huge slice of wild Africa on foot, camping by night in fly-tents pitched under shady trees or next to waterholes, and learning skills, such as tracking and stalking, that most of mankind has long forgotten.

Left: Waterbuck look on as a pair of young bull elephant spar playfully among the baobab trees of Tarangire National Park.

Kikoti Camp

The Maasai place of shelter

Kikoti Camp is built in a 10,000 acre game sanctuary in the Tarangire migration corridor, directly in the route of the vast herds of elephant that trek into the National Park in search of the permanent waters of the Tarangire River during the dry season. During the rainy season of November-January, the elephant herds trek back through Kikoti's land to disperse over the surrounding area, known as Maasailand after the Maasai pastoralists who are the original inhabitants of this part of Tanzania. Kikoti is a Maasai word meaning 'place of shelter' and is the name given to a huge granite kopje, or outcrop, under which warriors returning from cattle raids used to seek refuge with their stolen animals.

Kikoti is a low-key, unpretentious camp of just ten permanent tents, built by its camp staff, set into the hillside and designed to blend in its natural environment. Rather than the more traditional green canvas, Kikoti's tents are tawny brown in colour, in keeping with the muted browns of the dry grass and trees that surround them for most of the year. Each tent is built on a wooden platform, with a private verandah area outside and a palm-thatch roof overhead. The tents are simple and yet palatial, with ensuite bathrooms and double beds draped in romantic mosquito netting.

The camp's dining and lounge area is similarly simple, with bamboo and cane colonial furniture brightened up by bright green and blue cushions and decorated with Maasai artwork such as beaded necklaces and drinking gourds. Traditional Tanzanian ebony carvings of warriors and women offset the colonial feel and provide a reminder that Kikoti's atmosphere is heavily influenced by the ethnic culture of its surrounding area. Outside the dining room, a pleasant sandy fire area is dotted with bird baths created from lumps of granite, and food is put out daily for the flocks of iridescent starlings, red and white hornbills and bright green lovebirds that arrive daily to flutter in the water.

Being outside the official national park boundary, Kikoti's emphasis is on activities that differ slightly from the usual tourist game-viewing circuit. Guests here can walk in the surrounding area in search of prehistoric rock paintings, climb the nearby rocky outcrops to watch sunrise and sunset, or follow elephant paths to nearby waterholes. Night drives are arranged to see the bush from a totally different perspective and spot species not easily seen during the daytime such as bushbabies, civets or even the occasional leopard.

Kikoti is also committed to providing guests with a genuine and uncontrived insight into the culture of the Maasai people. Evening banquets are held in the camp's own *boma*, a circle of jagged wooden fencing originally designed to keep cattle safe from marauding lion. At Kikoti, however, the *boma* provides a venue for tables draped with bright red *shuka* blankets and set around a roaring fire, and meals accompanied by traditional songs and dances from the Maasai camp staff.

Left: The elegant open-sided lounge at Kikoti Camp, furnished with comfortable planters' chairs and cream cotton cushions.

Left: 'Maurice', a sculpture based on the blind Makonde drummer who became a national Tanzanian icon after mastering the art of playing twelve drums at once!
Above: A mosquito-net draped double bed is the centrepiece of each elevated tent at Kikoti.

Oliver's Camp

Walking in the wilderness zone

Paul Oliver, one of Africa's most experienced wildlife guides, has been leading safaris in Tanzania for more than twenty years. Recently relocated to a remote and beautiful corner of the park, far from any sign of human development, Oliver's Camp is a mecca for serious wildlife enthusiasts and safari connoisseurs from all over the world.

Oliver's new camp is sited in the so-called 'semi-wilderness zone' of Tarangire, a part of the park designated for special protection and in which no permanent structures of concrete or brick are allowed to damage the fragile ecosystem. The camp, entirely composed of traditional canvas tents, is set on an acacia-clad ridge overlooking the vast expanse of the Lanerkau and Silale swamps, a wildlife paradise in which herds of two or three hundred elephant are often seen feeding together, knee-deep in the long grass. To the east of Oliver's new location are the Simanjiro Plains, the birthing ground for Tarangire's vast herds of wildebeest and zebra, a spectacle which occurs each January and which rivals the better-known Serengeti migration for excitement and drama.

Oliver's seven bedrooom tents are sited well apart from each other and from the main camp to ensure that guests get that essential feeling of being deep in the bush, undisturbed by other signs of human life. The tents are large enough to be luxurious, with solid wooden furniture and the best cotton bedlinen, but small enough to blend in perfectly with the spectacular natural scenery and to seem dwarfed by the vastness of the surrounding landscape. The tents face the sunrise, meaning that most days begin with a pre-dawn wake up call and a cup of tea taken contemplating the streaks of crimson sky that appear as the sun makes its way up from behind the surrounding hills.

Oliver's Camp is elegant and stylish, but unpretentiously designed to provide pleasant and atmospheric surroundings for the real purpose of any visit – a true wilderness experience. Guests are encouraged to leave their vehicles behind and walk through the park for at least part of their stay, learning as they do about all too easily forgotten details such as grasses, insects, birds and reptiles, and developing bush skills such as tracking and stalking from Paul himself or one of the camp's other expert and inspirational guides. Mammal sightings around the camp are diverse and fascinating – alongside elephant, zebra and hartebeest are rarer species such as fringe-horned oryx or lesser kudu, as well as the resident cheetah that hunt on the ridge.

At the end of a day spent out in the bush dispensing knowledge, the Oliver's team are quick to provide guests with all the comforts that the old-fashioned white hunters considered essential for their well-heeled clients – a fine wine cellar, catching the evening light as it lies in a wooden rack; ice clinking in a cold gin-and-tonic; hot water carried carefully to each tent at sunset, and finally, a formal candlelit dinner, with safari stories flying around the table as the moon rises over the surrounding plains and night creatures rustle in the grass.

Left: The dining table at Oliver's Camp, scene of many a convivial evening.

Above: The comfortable chairs and coffee table of the mess are positioned to catch the golden light of Tarangire's famous sunsets.
Right: Oliver's mess area holds bowls of skulls, feathers and seed pods brought home by Paul from his walking safaris, alongside old-fashioned hurricane lamps for the evening.

Swala Camp
E a t i n g   w i t h   e l e p h a n t s

The silver cutlery and white table linen is gleaming in the sunlight, canvas chairs are drawn up comfortably on the verandah, and the ice chinks gently in the silver wine bucket. So far, just another leisurely lunch in the bush. But here at Swala there's a twist. Look up from buttering your bread roll and you'll find yourself eyeball to eyeball with a teenage bull elephant, his stentorian breathing almost fluttering the table napkins and his pungent, earthy smell competing with the aroma of basil and tomato rising from the plate in front of you. With a grunting bellow, shockingly loud at such close quarters, and his ears spread wide, he lurches towards you, trunk raised. But don't panic just yet. He's merely making way for another, more senior bull who has come up alongside to drink at the camp's waterhole, just yards away from the low terrace that surrounds Swala's elegant dining mess. During the dry season, the ten thousand litres of water pumped daily into the camp's waterholes ensure a guaranteed drink for a permanent herd of twenty or so elephants, as well as guaranteed once-in-a-lifetime game sightings for the camp's guests.

Once the initial thrill of close-up elephant contact has worn off slightly, there's plenty more at Swala to captivate even the most hardened cynic. Shyer bushbuck, with elegantly spiralling horns and huge, dewy eyes above wet black noses, take their turn at the water, ears twitching gently as they cautiously lower their heads to drink. Impala, even further down the pecking order, stay on the fringes, bobbing delicately around on impossibly fragile looking legs. And in the trees above, a panoply of birds flutter in the shady branches – a flash of purple announces a lilac-breasted roller, and an iridescent starling perches on the terrace railing, head cocked insolently.

Away from the verandah and its incredible animal interaction is the library, a comfortable, relaxing space of easy chairs and animal books. At the other end of the mess area is the formal dining room, magnificently furnished and lit, the dining table decorated with crystal glassware and innovative silver-coloured plates featuring elephants, appropriately, marching around the rim. These and the matching napkin rings have an interesting environmental background – rather than real silver, they are actually recycled aluminium, made from old coca-cola cans by a project in Zimbabwe.

Scattered around the dining tent are Swala's bedroom tents, each one furnished in the grand old fashioned safari style, with polished wood dressing tables, heavy trunks in place of bedside tables and Edwardian-style bathrooms, all brass taps, white porcelain and hurricane lamps. Thick Persian rugs cover the floor, and heavy linen curtains are held back with lengths of Maasai beadwork.

Outside each tent is a private verandah with comfortable canvas chairs, the better to watch the elephant that drift past on their way to the waterhole, sometimes turning curiously as though to look inside. As evening falls, the tent verandahs are the perfect place to find total peace and solitude, gazing out at the golden grasses of the Gurusi swamp as the shadows lengthen and the setting sun turns the dry red earth to shimmering copper.

Left: Lunch with an audience - Swala's resident herd of young bull elephants.

Left: The elegant dining table at Swala camp, with richly upholstered chairs in royal blue and gold.
Above: The polished wooden deck outside overlooks the camp watering hole.

Tarangire Treetops

Bedrooms in the branches

In the gently undulating landscape of the Tarangire National Park, one feature continually catches the eye – the enormous, squat shapes of giant baobab trees, their engorged trunks and strange, stubby branches giving the whole park an otherworldly, primeval character. Next to the gigantic trees even the huge tuskers for which the park is famous seem dwarfish.

Tarangire Treetops has taken this unassuming, even ugly tree and incorporated it into an innovative and exciting architectural scheme, with a series of 'treehouses' each built on stilts around the trunk of an ancient baobab. The trees lend their organic, timeless presence to the open sided rooms, which are constructed from local wood and pale golden straw thatch. Inside, cooling breezes blow through the open walls, with the burnt earth below showing through chinks in the polished wooden floorboards. Beds are constructed from rough timber, but finest Egyptian cotton sheets, warm quilts and woollen blankets make sure there is nothing uncomfortable about sleeping in a tree. At night, canvas flaps zip down snugly, with a window left open at the front to allow the sunrise light to filter in through the white, gauzy mosquito nets. Elephant drift past through the trees, oblivious to the humans gazing down from above.

In keeping with the intensely natural feel of the camp, wood is the prevailing theme in the interior design as well as the exterior architecture. The different textures of mankind's most fundamental building material are everywhere at Tarangire Treetops, the wooden structures moving gently in the wind or creaking under the impact of human footsteps. Rough bark clings to the twisted pillars that hold up the roof, knotted twigs are fashioned into light shades, and thick, heavy old doors have been salvaged and smoothed to become low tables in the bar. At the beginning and end of each day, the golden light lends quality to these myriad textures, fusing the created with the natural as the baobab trunks and the man-made structures blend together in organic harmony.

The central dining and bar areas of Tarangire Treetops are constructed around two massive baobabs, their gnarled trunks taking the place of interior walls. Wooden walkways connect the different levels of the space, with a relaxation area furnished with smart wooden safari chairs leading into a bar wrapped around the trunk of one of the trees, lumps of honey-coloured granite and silver dried grasses providing decoration and echoing the muted colours of Tarangire in the dry season – gold, tawny, russet and cream. The only hints of colour come from deep maroon woven cushions in the bar and a small plunge pool built into the decking, a flash of cool turquoise that suggests the vibrant greens and blue skies of Tarangire in the rainy season. After a swim in the hot afternoon, guests can relax with a sundowner and contemplate the elephants that arrive at dusk to drink from the waterhole, just metres from the terrace.

Left: The beds in Treetops' unique elevated bedrooms are constructed from rough timber, furnished with finest cotton sheets and warm woollen blankets.

Left and above: Maroon and leather chairs complement the natural colours of wood in Treetops' timber mess area, built around two massive baobab trees.

Above: A treehouse bedroom, hugging the massive trunk of a baobab and thatched with traditional *makuti* roofing.
Right: One corner of each bedroom is scattered with cushions for an afternoon spent relaxing or birdwatching.

 # Walking

'On foot, the pulse of Africa comes through your boot'

Peter Matthiessen, *The Tree Where Man was Born*

To walk in the African bush is, in the truest sense, to return to one's natural state. Mankind's first footsteps were taken on the plains of Africa, and our senses and minds evolved specifically to take us safely through this very landscape. The sights, smells and sounds of the African bush are deeply connected to our earliest memories, recalling the time when only human curiosity and adaptability ensured the survival of our ancestors.

To walk through the African bush is also to feel a connection with the old-time safari pioneers, the Europeans who came to Africa before the advent of roads or aeroplanes and opened up the bush the hard way - on foot. Their bush skills, and those of their guides, were all that kept them alive and brought them close to the animals they had come to see.

Walking is also a means of gaining access to wild areas unreachable by vehicle - steep sided gorges, river beds, high ridges - away from the roads and tracks that have been imposed over the centuries on the true landscape of Africa. The face of Africa is seen in closeup, with tiny details becoming as fascinating as the dramatic big game - the hole made by an ant lion, for example, or the life that teems inside a termite mound.

Tracks and signs, tiny noises and smells are all of paramount importance while watching wildlife in the bush. Only by means of specialist knowledge and exceptional powers of observation can animals be approached on foot - these skills cannot be learnt in any book but must be acquired slowly, through years of practice. Simply to walk quietly and without stumbling along a track littered with rocks, twigs and dry leaves is an activity that requires surprising amounts of concentration and practice - to do this while also keeping ears, eyes and nose alert to the possibility of big game nearby creates a rush of adrenaline as intense as in the wildest adventure sport.

Left: Viewing a herd of elephants on foot in the Selous Game Reserve.
Right: An evening walk from Sand Rivers Selous.

Lake Manyara National Park

Smaller and more low-key than its better-known neighbours, Lake Manyara National Park is a narrow strip of land tucked between the escarpment of the Great Rift Valley's eastern wall, and the soda-rich waters of Lake Manyara. The park is mainly covered with dense woodlands, watered by springs originating in the Ngorongoro Highlands, some of which are forced to the surface at temperatures exceeding 50 degrees centigrade. Perhaps because of its narrow breadth, Manyara has an otherwordly feel to it, the dark green, towering wall of the escarpment giving the impression of a lost kingdom, hidden from the outside world.

Lake Manyara can be a temperamental park, with the chilly bush on some grey mornings yielding little more than a few drab birds or perhaps a glimpse of mongoose tail disappearing into the bush. But as the sun warms the morning air and the clouds lift from the top of the escarpment, the enigmatic beauty of the ancient rock formations and the clear blue of the sky still lift the spirits like the wheeling kites that float on thermals across the cliffs.

Great flocks of flamingos appear periodically on the alkaline waters of the lake, disappearing overnight in search of new feeding grounds. Even without the flamingos, however, Lake Manyara is a bird-watcher's paradise, and even those with little interest in ornithology cannot fail to be captivated by the sight of a hundred white pelicans fishing together on the glassy blue surface of the lake, like a fleet of ocean-going ships. When dusk comes, the pink blush of the sky is reflected in the water, and the pelicans fly home, skimming the lake one behind the other in a great line.

Meanwhile, at twilight on the lake shore, a pride of lion climb into acacia trees, the great cats hanging limply like ripe golden fruit, while some of the park's huge elephant population take dust baths in a dry river bed below. Buffalo wade into the waters of the lake to cool off, remaining for hours still as statues and submerged to the neck. At the lake's edge, a lone, dun-coloured wildebeest stands, gazing wistfully towards the blue-grey hills on the other side as though dreaming of migration.

Left: Lake Manyara National Park's famous tree-climbing lions.

Lake Manyara Tree Lodge
Suites on stilts

Lake Manyara Tree Lodge is the latest venture from South African company CC Africa, a spectacular stilted lodge brought to fruition by architect Nick Plewman and interior designer Chris Browne. Plewman and Browne have worked together before, and find it hard to differentiate where one's job ends and the other's begins - the construction of the exteriors and the design of the interiors is so completely intertwined as to be inseparable.

The main lodge building is a soaring space built on different levels, rendered even more spectacular at night by the dozens of lanterns that illuminate it. It's a giant stage set affording sitting rooms, lounging areas, a store, an open-plan kitchen and a *boma*-style dining area. "It's a 21st-century take on the Elizabethan Globe Theatre," observes Browne, "plunked down in the heart of Africa." Each of the ten treehouses is mounted on stilts deep in the forest at the foot of the Rift Valley escarpment. The rooms are roofed with banana bark and comprise a sitting area, a bedroom dominated by a gauze-draped platform bed, a bathroom big enough for a cocktail party, a terrace nestling into the surrounding foliage, and a walk-in shower open to the night sky.

Browne scoured a dozen African countries to find the fabrics, textures, woods - and ideas - he needed to decorate his latest creation. The result is a design scheme simple enough to fit into the peaceful, leafy surrounds of the lakeside woodland, but also impeccably stylish down to the last tiny detail - from the bubbled brown glass sugar pots on the breakfast tray, to the fawn linen laundry bag in each bedroom, accompanied by a natural wood pencil and a laundry list made from rough, speckled brown paper.

Despite the plethora of tiny comforts that fill each space at Lake Manyara Tree Lodge, the design is very far from being inappropriately fussy and ornate for a lodge deep in the African bush. No brocade curtains or glass panes - instead the bedrooms are surrounded on all sides by a dozen mesh screens. Instead of pile carpets, floors at the Tree Lodge are made of smoothly sturdy, varnished lumber, helping to create a series of spaces which, though spectacular, are completely in harmony with the alluring environment that surrounds them.

Left: The *boma*-style dining area at Lake Manyara Tree Lodge.

Above and left: Lake Manyara Tree Lodge is built on stilts, bringing the sitting and sleeping areas almost level with the forest canopy.

Above and right: Impeccable attention to detail combines with a rustic, uncluttered feel to form the design scheme at Lake Manyara Tree Lodge.

Sokwe Mobile Camps

An old-fashioned private safari

"To depart on a safari is not only a physical act, it is also a gesture. You leave behind the worries, the strains, the irritations of life among people under pressure, and enter the world of creatures who are pressed into no moulds, but have only to be themselves; bonds loosen, anxiety fades, the mind closes against the world you left behind like a folding sea anemone."

Elspeth Huxley

The private tented, or 'mobile' safari is undoubtedly the most closely related modern experience to the first expeditions undertaken by the early hunters and adventurers who explored the unknown interior with a retinue of porters and staff. However exclusive, a camp or lodge will always have a slight tinge of the 'hotel' experience about it - the roads around it become well-known game trails, its boundaries unofficial 'fences' against the wilderness outside.

On a mobile safari, by contrast, the camp moves with the terrain, pitched for a few nights by a river bank to allow observation of species such as leopard or crocodile, then moved onto the open plains and surrounded by vast herds of herbivores like buffalo or wildebeest. Mobility is key, because it brings flexibility to game viewing - animals are unpredictable and their movements vary, with a location that's full of game one week being mysteriously empty the next. The secret is to have a camp designed to follow these mysterious movements, with a guide experienced enough to interpret the clues the animals leave behind and to catch up with them in their next port of call. A mobile safari can reach remote areas little known by the usual run of visitors, or go in pursuit of a single species in places far from the scope of a fixed-base safari.

With mobility, perhaps unexpectedly, comes comfort. Tanzania's modern mobile safari camps, such as those set up by Sokwe in Arusha, are massive operations involving every kind of luxury, moved on the back of heavy lorries ahead of clients in their game-watching cars. Tents are vast, roomy affairs, with private verandahs and en-suite bathrooms, and guests dine at night in a magnificent formal mess tent, the long table carefully laid with glass and porcelain and illuminated by candlelight. Groups of family or friends hire the entire camp operation for themselves, making an old-fashioned private safari in the style of the glamorous days of the 1930s and 40s.

After a hard day's walking or driving in search of game, Sokwe's camps have the feel of an oasis of civilisation and comfort in the midst of the bush. Decorative touches are brought in from the surrounding countryside - rocks, dried grasses, seed pods and flowers adorn the tents and dining areas, their muted browns and golds matching the camp's green glass bottles, beige khaki and undyed canvas. Sokwe's camps, for all their style, are designed to blend in seamlessly with the surrounding colours of the bush and not stand out brashly against the natural beauty that invariably surrounds them.

Left: The well-stocked dining table in a Sokwe mess tent.

Above and right: Mobile camping doesn't mean a compromise in comfort - Sokwe's mobile camps are more luxurious that many permanent ones.

Above and right: The sense of 'home' in the bush that Sokwe strives for in its mobile camps requires minute attention to a myriad of details.

Light in darkness

Early man probably discovered fire by accident, a gift from the heavens caused by a bolt of lightning striking a tree or a bush. It's entirely possible that this colossal step forward in the history of mankind happened in East Africa - even perhaps in modern-day Tanzania, where the oldest hominid footprints in the world reside, preserved by volcanic ash in Olduvai Gorge. If so, it's particularly appropriate that a campfire, lit for protection against the unknown dangers of the night, has become one of the most potent symbols of life in the African wilderness.

The dawning of a yellow flame, black soot shooting upwards against the pink tinge of a sunset, is a palpable sign that the long, hot day is over and the time for relaxation has begun. First a sundowner, a daily ritual to toast the passing of the sun's light and the advent of the fire. Then a meal, baked or grilled above the orange and white glow of charcoal embers. Lastly, a huddle of bodies around the dying remains of the fire, leaning forward to feed more wood to the flames or to pull a blanket closer around the shoulders. Some campfires are quiet circles of contemplation or just plain contentment, while others are raucous, hearty affairs with generous libations of liquor to fuel the telling of ever taller safari stories.

Robert Edwin Dietz, born in 1818 in New York City, is not one of the world's most famous inventors. But more than one safari hand should have reason to thank him - around 1850, Dietz was awarded a US patent for a new kind of lantern, designed specifically to burn a new fuel - kerosene. How Dietz's 'hurricane lamp' first came to East Africa is lost to history, but his creations, meticulously cleaned and filled anew each night, cast a soft glow over almost every safari evening.

Left: Hurricane lamps and a roaring fire illuminate a safari dinner table.
Right above: The fire is the focal point of any safari camp by night.
Below: Firelight flickers over the bottles of a mobile bush bar.

Selous Game Reserve

N amed after Frederick Courteney Selous, a Victorian hunter and naturalist, the Selous Game Reserve is one of the earth's last great wild places: 55,000 square kilometres of untamed bush, untouched forests, crocodile-filled lakes and emerald green floodplains. That's slightly larger than Switzerland, four times as big as the Serengeti, and the second biggest protected natural area in the world. Uninhabited since an outbreak of sleeping sickness evacuated the human population back in 1945, the Selous is one of the few places on earth, and certainly in Africa, that visitors can find utter, perfect solitude of the kind described by American author Peter Matthiessen in his bestseller *Sand Rivers*:

"Behind the heat and the still trees resounds the ringing that I hear when watched by something I cannot see. The power and the waiting in the air the stillness of the glittering water, the yellow water lilies and the tawny marsh grass, the circle of still trees that hide this lovely place from the outside world, the resounding silence and expectancy, as though the creatures of the earth's first morning might come two by two between the trees at any moment."

Walking through the Selous, in the same way as Matthiessen did, is harder work than driving, and doesn't provide the same number of 'instant hit' game sightings. But stick at it, and sooner or later you will be rewarded, perhaps, with a typical Selous encounter: the electric excitement of creeping towards a young bull elephant browsing in a patch of miombo woodland, closer and closer until you can hear his stentorian breathing and see the little midges that cluster in the corner of his eyes. Brown mud is caked on his skin, the edges of his ears are delicately ragged, and still the distance shortens until the life force of him seems to be right upon you, ears flapping suspiciously. It is at moments like these that the camera becomes an imposition, an obstacle that must be laid aside in favour of simply gaping with a foolish grin and pounding heart.

Boating is another highlight of any visit to the Selous - floating soundlessly among islands of half-submerged vegetation past the fish eagles perched on top of headless palm trees, standing in the flooded waters like totem poles. And at the end of the day, fly-camping next to the great brown sweep of the Rufiji River with just a mosquito net between the sleeper and the stars, nothing can disturb the feeling that one might be the first visitor, or even the first person, to come here - Adam or Eve, drifting off to sleep in the Garden of Eden.

Left: Sunset on the Rufiji River.

Sand Rivers Selous

T h e   l a s t   o f   O l d   A f r i c a

In the winter of 1980, a young safari outfitter from Kenya called Richard Bonham accompanied American writer Peter Matthiessen on an extended foot safari into the remote southern regions of the Selous Game Reserve, a massive tract of undeveloped and unpopulated land in southern Tanzania. It was the start of a love affair with the area Matthiessen had called 'the last of Old Africa', and Bonham, one of a breed more at home in the bush than the drawing room, returned to the Selous later in the 1980s to start a mobile safari operation, taking clients on old-style walking trips from a tented base camp.

Eventually it became apparent that the Selous, originally overlooked in favour of the more accessible northern parks of the Serengeti and Ngorongoro Crater, was becoming better known, and that the eyes of a large commercial operation were likely to fall upon it at any moment. Before this could happen, Bonham enlisted the help of two conservationist friends from Dar es Salaam, Lizzy and Bimb Theobald, and in 1984 building commenced on Sand Rivers, a tiny luxury lodge built of stone and ebony on a cliff high above the enormous *Heart of Darkness* expanse of the Rufiji river, the main artery of the Selous.

The eight cottages that Bonham built are simple, thatched affairs which have the front wall removed to allow guests to wake up, push back the mosquito net, and gaze from their bed at a yellow, green and blue expanse of river, bush and sky. The central space of the lodge is a magnificent dining and sitting area, built for panoramic views over a bend in the river, with a lagoon swimming pool set into the stone-flagged deck outside. At the end of the day, submerged up to the neck in the pool as the sunset sky turns purple, one can gaze almost eye to eye with a hippo, honking contentedly as it does the same in the river beyond.

The gentle, inexorable rush of the river is the soundtrack to everything that happens at Sand Rivers - the soft Swahili call of '*hodi*' from outside the door that announces morning tea, the buzz of insects from the trees in the heat of the afternoon, and the muffled roar of lion along its banks as darkness falls. After nineteen years, the site that Bonham chose for Sand Rivers still has the largest and most beautiful concession in the whole of the Selous - a vast paradise of dry river beds, miombo woodland and floodplains that appear suddenly from the dense bush, sparkling emerald green in the aftermath of the rainy season and stretching away to lakes and hills in the far distance.

But despite the transition from simple tented base camp to luxury lodge, walking safaris are still at the heart of a stay at Sand Rivers. A walk can last an hour, or a couple of weeks - and for *Boys Own* fun, no Land Rover can compete. At the end of a hard day on foot in the bush, evening fly camps are another speciality - the orange flare of hurricane lamps and a burgeoning fire in the descending blue twilight, and a neat row of mosquito net squares set against the rolling hills and pink, lowering clouds. As Peter Matthiessen put it:

"Gazing out across the sweep of sunset water to the green plain of Africa beyond, I feel tired, warm and easy, and awash with content."

Left: The magnificent driftwood dining table at Sand Rivers was made from a single log, salvaged from the river.

Above: Dappled sunlight filtered through the surrounding trees falls on the thatched roof of one of Sand Rivers' wood and stone cottages.

Right: The bedrooms are open on one side to allow the sounds and smells of the bush into the interior. Magnificent carved beds face the dramatic sweep of the Rufiji River.

Above: The Selous was immortalised by American writer Peter Matthiessen in his acclaimed book *Sand Rivers*.
Right: A wicker rocking chair provides the perfect place to rest or read during the fierce heat of the day.

Left and above: As darkness falls, the hurricane lamps are lit, dots of light in the blue twilight.

Left: Sand Rivers' game viewing hide, a platform built around the trunk of a tree. Bedrolls are spread out and a cool box imported for a leisurely afternoon of beer, book and binoculars.

Above: The outside terrace, set high up on cliffs over the glittering expanse of the river.

Above and right: A fly camp set up on a sandbar - a neat line of mosquito nets, with a long trestle table to serve as a bar for sundowners.

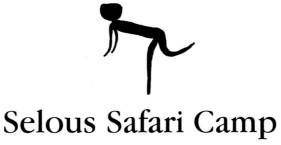

Selous Safari Camp

L o n g h o u s e s   o n   t h e   r i v e r   b a n k

Set on a flat, sandy stretch of bush next to a still bend in the Rufiji River, the Selous Safari Camp is dominated by the magnificent structure of its dining room and mess areas, inspired by the longhouses of Indonesia. Raised on stilts ten feet above the ground, the enormous *makuti* roofs cover interiors in which feminine details add a modern twist to the traditionally plain and masculine safari mess. Emphasis is given to creativity, inspired by the beauty of the surrounding landscape - two old-fashioned writing desks hold charcoal, canvas and watercolours, and the enormous leatherbound visitors' book is full of paintings and sketches by previous guests. Pride of place goes to an elegant watercolour of the river painted by HRH the Prince of Wales on a visit to the Selous in 1997. Homemade mobiles made from acacia thorns and hippo ivory hang along the massive pillars that support the structure in lieu of walls. Further decorative touches are provided by canoes and paddles, reflecting the proximity of the vast Rufiji river.

Tucked away in the trees around the towering mess are twelve elegant green canvas tents, raised on timber platforms, and a discreetly hidden swimming pool, kept cool by a roof of shade-cloth - a haven during the fierce heat of the afternoons. Each tent is thoughtfully designed and filled with dozens of small, yet essential luxuries - insect killer spray in a pale bamboo cover, wooden clothes hangers, and old-fashioned flasks holding chilled mineral water. Colours are muted, yet pretty - patterned cotton fabrics are used as bedcovers, and arrangements of brown and green dried flowers stand by the old-fashioned porcelain washbasins. Showers provide a sense of adventure, being situated outside the tents in green canvas shelters. During the dry season, a huge variety of big game wanders freely between the tents and around the mess area on the way to drink at the river - guests frequently report being awoken by the sound of giraffe stripping leaves from an acacia tree above their heads!

Out on game drives, the attention to detail that is the hallmark of the Selous Safari Camp operation is equally apparent. Softly purring petrol vehicles replace noisier diesel engines, and bucket seats, coolbox holders and handy pockets make spending all day in a Land Rover in search of elusive leopard or wild dog an effortlessly comfortable experience. Breakfast or dinner in the bush are sartorially elegant as well as delicious - polished wooden cutlery with bone handles, matching tablecloths and proper china crockery are *de rigeur*, even when picnicking next to crocodile-filled lakes. Morning coffee, one of safari's most unbreakable traditions, is likewise aesthetically pleasing - wooden trays, brass teapots, and elephant-shaped chocolate biscuits await the bleary-eyed guest stumbling out for a morning game drive.

Left: The mess area at Selous Safari Camp is raised on stilts, its vast, curved thatched roof based on the design of an Indonesian longhouse.

Above: An antique leather trunk doubles as a coffee table.

Right: Pink sofa covers and upholstery give a feminine edge to the traditionally masculine furnishings of the mess.

Above and right: The furnishings of Selous Safari Camp are a myriad of textures and materials - elegantly polished tables stand alongside homemade mobiles made from warthog tusks and acacia thorns, old canoe paddles are propped against the rope balconies, and tea and coffee arrives in wickerwork flasks.

Above and right: The traditional walk-in Selous tents are set among trees at the water's edge and furnished in muted beiges, browns and creams.

 # Boating

What greater pleasure than to wake early and spend the first hours of light messing about in a boat, chugging up the great muddy sweep of the Rufiji river, or paddling a canoe along the steamy shores of Lake Manyara? Baboons slope onto tumbled boulders to stare insolently and scratch their bottoms as you pass; hippo ease gently down in the water to watch your progress; fish eagles regard the boat contemplatively from low-hanging boughs. A leopard, glimpsed for a second lazing on rocks by the water's edge, flicks her tail irritably and vanishes into the shadows.

At the end of a boat ride, a picnic breakfast of bacon and egg sandwiches is eaten on a shallow sandy beach as the sun gears up for the day's heat. A giant kingfisher flies by low over the water, and the grunts of hippo come startlingly close from behind a rock.

On Lake Manyara, the shallow water recedes in diminishing ripples from the prow of a light fibreglass canoe, the afternoon sun sending lances of light down through the clouds to illuminate the feathers of thousands of flamingoes, wading through the water just metres away. Their harsh cries resonate around the high, dark green walls of the escarpment, which dwarfs both lake and canoe. Canoeing on the lake gives a different perspective to the park - the landscape is seen from the angle of a waterbird, peering between the legs of the elephant that emerge from the bush to drink, oblivious of the strange creature paddling silently past.

Left: top: A buffalo submerged among water weed in the Rufiji River.
Middle: Crocodiles emerge from the river by day to lie gaping on sandbanks.
Bottom: Flocks of birds fly over an evening canoe trip on Lake Manyara.
Right: Returning at sunset from a boat trip in the Selous Game Reserve.

Ruaha National Park

Ruaha National Park is Tanzania's second largest, a vast wilderness in the south-west of the country, visited by only a handful of travellers each year. At the park's heart is the well-named Great Ruaha River, a massive watercourse that dwindles to only a few pools in the dry season, but bursts its banks and roars over boulders at the height of the rains.

Converging with the Great Ruaha are hundreds of sand rivers, natural game corridors when dry and sparklingly clear streams when wet. Waterbuck, impala and the world's most southerly Grant's gazelle risk their lives for a sip of water - the shores of the Ruaha are a permanent hunting ground for lion, leopard, jackal, hyena and the rare and endangered African wild dog. Ruaha's elephants are recovering strongly from ivory poaching in the 1980s and remain the largest population in East Africa. Ruaha represents a transition zone where eastern and southern species of flora and fauna overlap - lesser and greater kudu co-exist with northern species such as Grant's gazelle.

Between the rivers lies a massive, completely unspoilt landscape of plains, rocky gullies, thick miombo woodland and distant purple hills. Ruaha is a dramatic park, its scenery ever-changing and full of detail - the white blossoms that appear on the bald, stark branches of baobab trees and the gigantic blue-black granite boulders that lie in tumbled plains in the river valleys.

This drama also extends to one episode in the area's history - Ruaha was the scene of the beginning of the Maji Maji (or 'water') rebellion, a widespread revolt in which various separate southern Tanzanian tribes rose up against their German overlords at the turn of the 20th century. The warriors who led their people into battle were protected by sacred water given to them by their charismatic spiritual leader Kinjikitile, who claimed that this water, mixed with millet flour and castor oil and sprinkled on the body, would cause the bullets of the enemy to have no effect. The water itself is believed to have come from a set of sacred springs that still bubble up in green, pungent swamps within the borders of the park.

Left: The magnificent black-maned lions of Ruaha National Park.

Jongomero

Elegance   at   the   river's   edge

Jongomero, Ruaha National Park's newest lodge, brings a sleek modern style to the classic design of a traditional tented safari camp. Situated on the bank of the Jongomero River, the camp's tall, pale straw roofs are the same golden yellow as the tawny grasses that cover the park during the dry season. Dappled sunlight falls onto them between the acacia and fig trees that grow along the river's edge, their startlingly green foliage contrasting sharply with the arid expanse of the riverbed, devoid of water for half the year.

The mess and dining areas, entered under the natural arch of a gigantic baobab branch, are built of sustainable eucalyptus wood, set on a cliff and looking down onto the natural game corridor of the river bed, where groups of elephant often appear in the dry heat of midday to dig for water in the sandy bottom. Open on all sides for maximum air circulation, they are joined by a ramp to add a sense of formality - guests walk up into the slightly elevated dining room to eat each evening.

The interiors of Jongomero's public spaces are free of clutter, the smooth wooden floors and comfortable sofas clean and welcoming after the riot of heat and colour of the park outside. The furniture, like the structure itself, has been built from sustainable wood sources, in this case old Swahili fishing dhows salvaged from the beaches of Dar es Salaam and planed smooth, revealing rich browns and blacks under the rotten, pitted wood of the surface.

The bedrooms at Jongomero are extremely smart safari tents, made from pale canvas to match the sand of the river bed, with the slatted wooden verandahs in front of each one reaching right to the river banks. Inside the colour scheme is similar to the rest of the camp in its simplicity - beige and black check bedcovers, pale wooden floors and brown leather easy chairs. The bathrooms are modern and funky, with stainless steel sinks set into wood and cast iron counters, old fashioned taps and piles of cream fluffy towels.

Building a new camp in an area unoccupied by man is always a challenge - the wild beauty of the Jongomero area needed to be shielded from any adverse effects associated with the presence of humans. The camp is designed to blend in as much as possible with the surrounding environment, and staff and guides are slowly winning the trust of the area's plentiful wild game, which includes greater kudu, roan and sable antelope as well as the rare African hunting dog. Jongomero is built in the heart of the territory of the resident lion pride, and the big cats are frequent visitors to the camp, with their roars echoing along the banks of the river as darkness falls each evening.

Left: Lunch outside on the flagstone verandah at Jongomero.

Above and right: The furniture at Jongomero is modern and sleek, complementing the smooth wooden floors and muted colours of the upholstery.

Mwagusi Safari Camp

A b u s h h o m e w i t h s t y l e

Tiny, private Mwagusi Safari Camp, nestling discreetly in the bush on the banks of the Mwagusi River, enjoys a reputation out of all proportion to its size. Mwagusi's fame as one of the most exciting bush camps in Africa is gained not by exterior trappings or a well-oiled publicity machine but by the expertise of its owner, Chris Fox. Having immersed himself in the life and ecosystems of the Ruaha National Park since his childhood, Chris is perfectly placed to lead his guests by vehicle or on foot to its most secret locations. His knowledge of the game in the vast area around his home means that once-in-a-lifetime wildlife experiences are almost commonplace for his guests - the chance to see harder to find species like cheetah, for example, or to have a close encounter with Constantine, the bull elephant with whom Chris has shared a lifetime friendship.

Mwagusi may be first and foremost a bush camp and a home, but the buildings themselves are nonetheless the equal of the most carefully designed hotel. Ineffably stylish, Mwagusi comprises a series of extravagant straw bandas - some winged like Sydney Opera House, some round and turreted like a medieval palladium. Grass stalks cut from meadows outside the park have been trimmed into equal lengths and set into wooden frames to be built into walls, shelves, dressing tables, armchairs, and even sofas.

The many and varied decorative touches come entirely from natural materials also - a dazzling textural variety of horns, skulls, snakeskins, pebbles and seed pods fill every surface. Great slabs of granite replace man-made benches; smooth hollow stones are used as washbasins, and towels hang from ebony branches set into the walls. The natural yellow and brown textures of all this organic decoration are vibrantly tempered by the rich red of the stained cement floor and the deep navy blue upholstery on the chairs and sofas, brightened still further by smart tartan cushions in royal blue and red check.

The bedrooms at Mwagusi are a funky and innovative take on the traditional 'boy scout' feel of a tented safari camp. Each traditional green canvas tent is entirely enclosed in a straw pavilion, with a vast bathroom built onto the back. In front is a sand-floored sitting room, divided from the main bedroom by a low straw wall into which two huge, comfortable armchairs have been built, their thick cushions providing the perfect place to collapse and contemplate the vista of river, bush and sky that is framed by the open wall in front. At night, the core tent is zipped up to provide protection from insects and curious animals, the sheer mosquito netting walls transparent enough to allow the moonlight to filter in alongside the distant roar of lion, and the sound of elephant feeding in the riverbed just outside.

Left: The mess area at Mwagusi - low sofas built of straw are topped with dark blue upholstery and brightly coloured cushions.

Left: An encounter with Constantine, the bull elephant with whom Chris Fox has shared several years of friendship.
Above: Slightly more static elephants, sculpted by Michael Ghauri.

Above and right: Organic materials form sofas, washstands, tables and ornaments at Mwagusi, bringing the textures and colours of the bush into the design scheme of the interiors.

Above: A flamboyant, medieval-style pavilion roof tops the library.
Right: Dinner in the dry bed of the Mwagusi sand river.

Left and above: Each traditional green canvas bedroom tent is surrounded by an extravagent straw pavilion, with easy chairs on the sand-floored private verandah and smart checked bedspreads.

Above and right: A giraffe skull and neck vertebrae top the low stone wall in this bathroom - organic materials such as bones and skulls are very much part of the design scheme at Mwagusi.

Ruaha River Lodge

Buffalo, baobabs and boulders

One of Tanzania's longest-established safari lodges, Ruaha River Lodge was set up by tea farmer Geoff Fox and his wife Vicky in the 1970s. The Fox family have been deeply involved with the park ever since, founding the Friends of Ruaha Society to support the conservation work of the game rangers and the park authorities. The lodge is now run by the second generation of the family, Peter Fox and his wife Sarah. The Foxes, however, were far from being the first inhabitants of the area - Stone Age tools and weapons have been found close to the site of the lodge, suggesting that the essential waters of the Ruaha River have supported the existence of humans since their first days on earth.

Overlooking a magnificent bend in the river, the lodge is built on two levels, with one section along the edge of the boulder-strewn riverbed, and another etched into the granite of the kopjes themselves further up the cliffs. Both the main camp and the river camp blend seamlessly into their environment, with the whole lodge being almost invisible to the approaching visitor until the very moment of arrival.

The different positions of Ruaha's two camps give very different perspectives on the wild game that abounds in and around the lodge - the riverfront bedrooms are metres away from the water, with impala, waterbuck and even lion passing in front of the buildings on their way to drink. Further up the hill, the main camp bar, entered through a crack in the rockface, has a panoramic view of the whole southern part of the Ruaha National Park, with its massive herds of buffalo passing through the stands of acacia and baobab trees that grow on the far bank of the river.

The banda bedrooms are cool and airy, with wire mesh in place of glass windows to allow the breeze to pass through. Each has a small private verandah for watching the animal action along the river, and the interior is decorated simply with pretty wooden bowls of dried flowers and seedpods gathered from the surrounding bush. The public bars and dining rooms at both camps are straw-thatched and open-sided, with honeycombs and weaver birds' nests among the wildlife paintings on the walls, and buffalo and giraffe skulls guarding the entrances.

The riverbed itself is the focus of the lodge, with all the structures facing down into the Ruaha River, which in the wet season bubbles and eddies past the boulders on its bottom, and in the dry season shrinks to a few small pools of water in which flocks of storks and egrets gather, chasing catfish to and fro with bills clattering among the cautious waterbuck and impala that come out of the bush to drink.

Many of Ruaha River Camp's visitors are expatriates and locals from Dar es Salaam or Iringa, looking not for a contrived tourist experience but for an unspoilt wilderness and a friendly base from which to drive out in search of Ruaha's plentiful wild game. This local flavour gives the camp a friendly, unpretentious feel, with the stunning natural environment taking priority over any imposed design scheme or showy architecture.

Left: The buildings at Ruaha River Lodge blend seamlessly into their riverside environment.

Left and above: Each banda has small private verandah for watching the animal action along the Ruaha River, with giraffe and buffalo skulls guarding the entrances.

Above: The river bar at Ruaha River Lodge is just metres from the water's edge, with animals passing close by on their way to drink.

Right: The kopje bar is literally squeezed into a crack in the granite rockface, high above the river.

Old safari hands

Every colonial land has its legends - men and women who arrived from elsewhere and made their mark through courage, sporting prowess or simply style. Tanganyika had its heroes and eccentrics too - fighting, shooting or partying their way into the history books.

Frederick Courtenay Selous

Selous arrived in South Africa in 1871, aged 19, equipped only with £400 and a heavy rifle. He quickly became the most celebrated hunter of his generation, a true Victorian hero and the model for H Rider Haggard's fictional hero Allan Quatermain. At sixty-three he returned to serve in East Africa in the Great War; he was shot by a sniper while commanding his 'Legion of Frontiersmen' in the area that is now named after him - the Selous Game Reserve.

JA Hunter

John Alexander Hunter was one of the greatest professional hunters the colonies of British and German East Africa had ever seen, respected by clients and fellow sportsmen alike. Shooting on game control assignments as well as tourist safaris, Hunter probably shot more 'big five' game than any other - in a career spanning 50 years, he shot 1,000 rhinoceros and 1,400 elephant. Later in life, like many old-time professional hunters, he became a conservationist, serving as a game warden in Kenya. He was also fond of the wild territory that later became Tanganyika, and was once offered the Ngorongoro Crater for £16!

Bror (and Cockie) von Blixen-Finecke

The erstwhile husband of Karen Blixen, 'Blix' was renowned throughout East Africa as 'the toughest, most durable white hunter ever to shoot a charging buffalo between the eyes while debating whether his sundowner will be gin or whiskey'. He met his match in his second wife Cockie, a formidable socialite with a wit and energy to match his own. The couple moved to Tanganyika and set up home in a tin shack near Babati, entertaining the Prince of Wales to scrambled eggs and gin when he arrived on safari in 1928.

Left: Frederick Courtenay Selous.
Right above: An early edition of JA Hunter's memoirs.
below: A Bror Blixen safari in full swing.

A1391

A BANTAM GIANT 35¢

HUNTER

The amazing true adventures of Africa's greatest white hunter . . . "There will never be a book written to beat it." SATURDAY REVIEW

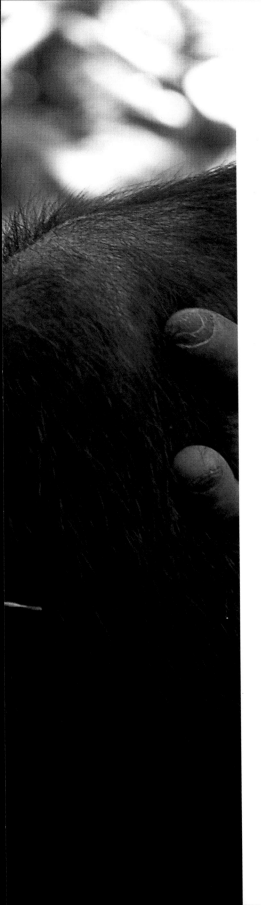

Mahale National Park

The green-carpeted mountains rise dramatically into the sky, their tops wisped with steamy clouds. Eagles wheel across the peaks, the sacred burial grounds of Tongwe chiefs. Deep in the forest, with its trailing vines and tangled creepers, a high, shrieking hoot is heard, followed by a wild screaming and a deafening crash of branches. Suddenly a chimpanzee appears on the rock-strewn path, teeth bared defensively and massive shoulders hunched in aggression. This is the alpha male of the group, Fenana, making his presence felt to the fifty or so chimps that are presently feeding in this part of the forest. He breaks off a branch and charges, flailing the leaves around his head in a wild display of power. The second and third ranking males, who had been enjoying a nap in a pool of sunshine at the edge of the trees, hastily make way, shrieking placatingly and stretching their mouths into deferential smiles.

Unconcerned by the din, an elderly female and a young adolescent clasp each other's hands above their heads as they painstakingly groom the skin parasites from their armpits. A young female with a baby appears suddenly from the undergrowth - as she joins in the grooming, her baby jumps down from his jockey-style position on her back and amuses himself turning somersaults and chasing the giant blue butterflies that flutter past in the shafts of sunlight that filter down through the trees.

Just another ordinary day for the Japanese research team who have been studying this group of chimpanzees continually since 1965, doing work just as valuable as their better-known neighbour, Jane Goodall, a few hundred kilometres away in Gombe Stream. Thanks to their work, the chimpanzees, while still 100% wild, are fully habituated to human beings, and can be joined by small groups of visitors, who make the steep climb up through the humid forest to the apes' domain. Untroubled by their observers, the chimps play out their family struggles and political campaigns in the safety of the National Park forest, demonstrating behaviour that shows how closely related they are to humans as they strip twigs to use as tools and hunt monkeys or bushpigs for meat, sharing out the spoils according to a complicated social system. Visitors can squat unnoticed on pathways as the chimps nurse and play with their offspring, squabble among themselves over the choicest fruits and berries, or build nests of leaves and twigs in the treetops for a tranquil afternoon nap.

Walking in the forest, with the turquoise waters of Lake Tanganyika twinkling tantalisingly through the trees far below, is sweaty, humid work. But an hour or two observing the chimpanzees going about their business, waiting breathlessly for the upshot of a hunt, or pressing oneself back into the bushes as a big male shoots by, is one of the most profound experiences to be had anywhere. And after the sweaty exertions of the morning, the clear, fresh waters of the lake beckon, fringed with beaches pristine enough to rival any on earth.

Left: A male chimp takes a midday nap on a forest path in the Mahale Mountains National Park.

Greystoke Camp

Any primate's paradise

There are few places in the world as achingly beautiful as Kangwena Beach, one of the chain of bays that fringe the edge of Lake Tanganyika close to where Henry Morton Stanley pitched camp in 1876 during his legendary crossing of Africa from east to west. Soft white sand slopes gently towards the endless shimmer of the turquoise lake, a body of water so pure that the hippos that live along its shores can be clearly seen walking along the bottom. Floating in the water, one can look back beyond the beach to the towering hills, covered with green forest, which reach up into the wisps of cloud far above. Over the gentle lapping of the water, the screech of exotic birds wafts faintly back from the shore, accompanied on occasion by the unearthly, primeval hoots and shrieks of the chimpanzees that rule the forest.

To put a camp in an Eden like this is a fearsome responsibility - it must be as perfect as the glittering lake, as relaxed as the rhythms of the forest. As Roland Purcell, the camp's creator, puts it: "If I dare to put an imprint on this paradise, I'd better get it right."

Greystoke camp is irresistibly, magically right. Six double tents, simply furnished, pitched slightly back into the whispering palms at the edge of the beach. Forest bathrooms with suspended bucket showers set among the trees, or perhaps a bath taken in the lake, rinsing out soap suds while gazing back at the misty peaks. The mess tent is a sculptured palace of wood, canvas and thatch, modeled on the design of a Tongwe chief's hut and decorated inside by drapes of unbleached cotton and freshly picked green palm fronds. A ladder leads up to the cool mezzanine floor, with overloaded bookshelves standing under the eaves among scattered cushions on which to nest, like a chimp in a tree, during the heat of the day.

Every morning, while the air is still cool, guests trek into the forest, a magical kingdom of sunlit ferns, dangling creepers and still pools above smooth scattered boulders. The chimpanzees lead one on, their wild calls first tantalizingly close then echoingly distant, as the paths grow steeper and narrower. They appear finally, habituated to humans, relaxed, confident and fascinating. Two hours in their company goes too fast, and the forest is left behind once again for the glare of the beach and the green coolness of the lake.

Afternoons are spent lazing in oversized deckchairs or floating indolently in the water, until the sun sets in ribbons of gold over the lake's surface and the mess tent glows against the dark green mountains like a great jewel. As the air grows cooler, a fishing trip beckons in the camp's 45 foot sailing dhow, the *Isabella*, reclining on cushions while eating lake-fresh sashimi as the glassy twilight water slips along the hull. At night, when the lights of Congo twinkle in the distance, the drama of the camp's setting is enhanced by the great dining table set out on the sand, surrounded by flares and lit from above by the moon and stars.

Left: The great chief's tent of the mess at Greystoke Camp is the backdrop for dinner outside on the beach, dramatically lit by flares.

Above: Rich red and gold cushions are scattered on the mess's mezzanine floor.
Right: The Greystoke mess tent in daylight, dwarfed by the vast dark green hills behind.

Left: Lunch is set in the cool interior of the mess tent, draped in cream canvas and decorated with freshly-cut palm fronds.
Above: A glass of Pimms at sundowner time, looking out over the lake.

Above: 'fish-friendly' biodegradable shampoo and conditioner are provided in elegant blue glass bottles for washing in the lake.
Right: The *Isabella*, Greystoke's 45-foot long sailing dhow.

Left: Greystoke's simple tents are set back into the whispering forest at the beach's edge.
Above: Old-fashioned bucket showers stand among the oil palm trees behind each tent.

 # Food & cooking

'An army marches on its stomach'. This saying could also hold true for a safari. Since the times of the earliest pioneers, food and cooking have been an integral part of the safari experience. Livingstone and Burton may have had to exist on termites and grubs as they forged their way into the nineteenth century unknown, but ever since the continent became the playground of Europe's rich and famous in the early twentieth century, food standards on safari have been becoming ever more lavish. The white hunters of the 1930s considered it shockingly lax to entertain their film-star and industrialist clients with anything less than ten courses at dinner, all conjured from supplies carried laboriously on the heads of porters, or gleaned from game shot along the way.

These days safari cuisine has become more influenced by the flavours of the continent itself. African food is bold and colourful, with rich, earthy textures and strong, spicy undertones. Arab merchants, European colonists and Malay slaves have all influenced Africa's native cooking, resulting in a cuisine diverse and yet simple to prepare. But whether fly-camping in the bush or staying in a lodge, the day still begins with the traditional 'Full English' - bacon, sausages, tomato and fried eggs, more often than not cooked in a heavy iron skillet over a wood fire before dawn by the camp cooks. Fresh tropical fruits from the lowlands and hardy vegetables from cool highlands are always available.

Bush chefs work miracles with the most basic of equipment and ingredients - fresh baked bread is prepared in an old tin trunk over smouldering ashes, legs of succulent lamb are roasted by being buried in the earth in a nest of hot coals, or vegetable kebabs skewered on pieces of wood plucked from a nearby tree. Food is kept cold in gas fridges, packed in ice or simply brought into camp "on the hoof"!

Left above: Putting the final touches to a bush dinner at Klein's Camp in the Serengeti.
Below: Breakfast on the beach at Greystoke Camp, Mahale Mountains National Park.
Right: A picnic table is spread with Maasai cloth for a safari breakfast.

Katavi National Park

T he million acre Katavi National Park in western Tanzania is a place for the safari connoisseur - the African insiders' destination of choice. The tiny number of visitors who arrive have worked hard to get there - a four-hour flight in a tiny Cessna, or five days' bumping along potholed roads in a Land Rover. But the reward is a perfect, unspoilt wilderness where rules are left far behind - one can set off on foot along river banks, or track game cross-country across the plains in any direction, far from the nearest road.

In streams, creeks and muddy pools, hundreds of hippo lie packed together, their silage smell thickening the air and the marshlands resounding with their symphony of grunts and snorts. Calves wallow next to their obese mothers, tiny, unformed snouts resting along the backs of their elders to avoid being squashed into the mire. The hippos of Katavi don't huddle defensively in the water during daylight hours, as though besieged - so confident are they in their vast habitat that they roam the plains contentedly in the sunlight, trotting purposefully across the grass between the rivers.

It is fitting that the crocodile, that most prehistoric of reptiles, thrives in the primeval atmosphere of Katavi. The slim, yellow and brown spotted females wriggle on their bellies up the riverbanks to sunbathe, skidding back into the river at the first sign of disturbance. The larger, thick-skinned males slither in and out of the holes they've excavated in the soft mud, gimlet eyes coldly surveying the muddy waters for prey.

Away from the plains, in Katavi's sun-dappled, mysterious woodlands, white cape chestnut trees glow among the acacias and wild figs. A moving mass of shadow becomes a herd of elephant, padding silently along between the trees on their way to the plains, relaxed trunks swinging like pendulums between their forelegs. The silent, graceful form of a giraffe sways away in alarm across a clearing, and on rare, lucky occasions, the honey-coloured shape of a rare puku antelope is glimpsed at the edge of the trees.

Driving in dry season across the primeval swamplands, with the dry leaves of Borassus palm trees rustling eerily in the wind, it's easy to believe one has entered a lost world, a world in which the beasts rule and man is merely another, rather insignificant mammal, tolerated only at the mercy of the animals. Massive herds of buffalo, visible in the distance as an endless line of black dots wavering in the heat haze, scatter across the yellow dry season grasses. Prides of lion, glutted with prey, roar in the darkness every night. The lack of human visitors in Katavi means that the game is still as wild as it was at the dawn of time. The elephant still charge, the impala still leap gracefully into the air as they skitter away through the trees at the approach of a human. This is Africa as it once was - pure, wild and endlessly exciting.

Left: Katavi's vast hippo population congregate in ever-dwindling pools of muddy water as the dry season progresses.

Chada Camp

S i x   t e n t s   i n   a   m i l l i o n   a c r e s

If Katavi is the Africa insider's park, Chada is definitely the connoisseur's safari camp. Six tents in a million acres of wild game - it doesn't get much more exclusive than this. And those who make the pilgrimage to Chada are not concerned with window dressing; they've seen it all before. Roland and Zoe Purcell have created their camp to be as inconspicuous as possible - just a few visitors at a time are flown in by Roland in his Cessna 206, skimming low across the vast herds of buffalo and the hippo-filled rivers before bumping down on an airstrip frequently shared with giraffe, antelope or elephant. A short drive through the woodland brings one into camp - an arrival heralded by the smell of woodsmoke and the clink of ice in a gin and tonic as the sun sets over the plain. The style of Chada is rugged and masculine, unconsciously elegant and unadorned. The camp has comforts in abundance - feather pillows, ice cold drinks, steaming hot showers - but, as Roland puts it, "They're not really the point".

This is a place far from civilisation - in the absence of technology or bottled entertainment, the lost art of conversation is regained at lunch under the trees or dinner by lamplight in the mess tent. Stories fly, the world is set to rights, laughter fills the dark air. Books, too, are important - Chada's impressive library covers all subjects from natural history to eastern philosophy, all to be enjoyed during the quiet of a still afternoon as the heat haze dances across the plain.

Chada's tents are beige canvas, simply furnished with handmade wooden cots, spread with colourful kikoi covers to keep out the night chill. Bathrooms are outside, canvas bucket showers suspended from the branches of fig trees. The tent fronts unzip to a vista like the Garden of Eden - the huge Chada flood-plain which surrounds the camp on three sides, providing a panorama of wild Africa without the need to move an inch. Zebra wade knee-deep in the yellow grasses, ears flicking at flies; a file of elephant move slowly past in the middle distance; and just visible through the haze, great herds of buffalo congregate, an indistinct row of shapes on the horizon.

Visitors to Chada can choose, spontaneously, between a walk along the river bank, creeping up on a flock of vultures bathing in the muddy water, or perhaps a drive across the plains, pitted and rutted with the mud of a thousand buffalo footprints, to spy on the prides of lion who follow the great herbivores day and night. An exotic picnic table is brought into a stand of Borassus palms, canvas deckchairs and cushions spread out for an afternoon nap overlooking a waterhole. Or perhaps the decision is made to leave the camp behind altogether, spread out bedrolls under the stars, and settle down for a nights' sleep soothed by the wind through the branches and the piping of night birds. At Chada, anything goes - rules are in short supply. But surely that's the idea of a stay in the wilderness?

Left: Chada's camp furniture is simple and functional - canvas campaign chairs, well-thumbed books, and an antique telescope for scanning the surrounding plains.

Above: There are no fences or borders at Chada - tents are pitched facing the panoramic vista of the Chada floodplain, with game wandering through the camp day and night.
Right: Chada is not a camp that proclaims itself 'luxurious', but despite this, dozens of savvy details ensure comfort as well as an easy, effortless style.

Fly camping

'Fly camp' as a term refers to a small, light and temporary camp set up deep in the bush for a night or two then moved again next day, leaving behind only the ashes of a campfire. Fly camps can be set up for any purpose, but usually accompany walking safaris, with camp staff or porters going on ahead to set up camp and welcome weary trekkers with a cold gin and tonic at the end of the day.

Fly camp style is all about details - a little mirror hangs with a green towel next to each folding canvas washstand, or a shower made from a khaki bag bulging with hot water, slung over a low hanging tree branch, a bar of soap wedged conveniently into a hippo skull. A thousand miles of wilderness retreat from beyond the neat little loo seat, set on a cliff or at a river's edge.

Dinner is served at a long table drawn up next to the reassurance of the campfire, moths dancing in the light of hurricane lamps as three courses of miraculously fine cuisine, prepared on nothing more than a wood fire, are served to the accompaniment of shrilling insects, the scent of smoke and the crackle of burning logs. After dinner is the time to sit around the fire and tell stories, or perhaps just listen to the distant roaring of lions, before retiring early to sleep.

Tents are optional - fly camps often consist only of a mosquito net set up around a mattress, in a bush clearing or perhaps under a baobab tree. The stars are visible from one's pillow, and the night noises of Africa are the background to sleep. Nothing brings the experience of Africa closer, no luxury camp can provide the same level of excitement as just one night spent sleeping on the earth in the heart of the bush.

Left: A fly camping trip from Oliver's Camp in Tarangire National Park.
Right: The ubiquitous canvas bucket shower.

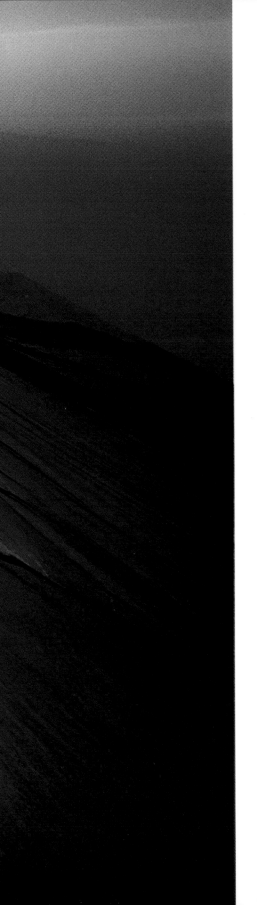

Arusha

European settlement in the Arusha area began in 1896, when a German captain, Kurt Johannes, approached the waArusha tribe living around the base of Mount Meru in an attempt to secure diplomatic relations with local chiefs. But the waArusha warriors, unable to forget a German raid of the previous year, attacked and killed two missionaries. Captain Johannes duly returned to his base in Moshi, mobilized Chagga troops and returned to inflict a punishing victory. In 1899 the Germans began construction of a strong fortification, a *boma*, which they forced the waArusha to build.

A steady influx of traders and farmers moved into Arusha in the 19th century, including Indian traders and German farmers. The new arrivals stimulated economic growth, and in the early twentieth century Arusha grew into a pleasant destination for the bolder safari clients who set out from Nairobi with their white hunters. Unlike Nairobi's flat landscape, Arusha was sited at the base of Mount Meru, amid rolling green foothills and lush forests, more reminiscent of the Alps than the tropics. The town boasted one tiny hotel, known as Blooms, where hardy German settlers gathered to drink and carouse alongside a few British residents, and passing hunters sipped gin and tonic in the bar. Arusha remained a small hunting and farming community, surrounded by vast wheat and grain farming regions on the slopes of Kilimanjaro. Like Nairobi, the settlement retained a 'wild west' flavour until well into the 20th century, but unlike its Kenyan counterpart, Arusha was not predominantly British, but had a more international flavour.

One of the most important figures in the history of Tanganyika, as the colony became known after the First World War, was Kenyon Painter, , a wealthy American businessman who first came to Arusha on a safari in 1907. Painter returned to the town to invest 11 million dollars in a coffee estate, factory and experimental research centre, as well as building the New Arusha Hotel, one of the region's most famous buildings. The front of the hotel boasted a sign saying: *This spot is exactly half way between the Cape and Cairo and the exact centre of Kenya, Uganda, and Tanganyika.*

Today, although Arusha's central position on the continent remains unchanged, most of the town, with its hardware shops, curio stalls and internet cafes, would be unrecognisable to the farmers and white hunters who lived there in its formative years. Away from the hustle and bustle of the town centre, however, still lie a few small highland settlements that seem to have changed very little since the early years of the twentieth century - pockets of tranquillity where mountain streams rush through forested valleys, steep paths rise up past banana and coconut plantations, and neat rows of coffee plants bisect green hillsides.

Left: Mount Meru's blue-grey cone towers on the horizon opposite its more famous neighbour, Kilimanjaro.

Ngare Sero Mountain Lodge
Fortress turned country house

Strange as it may seem, the tranquil German farmhouse of Ngare Sero was originally conceived as a kind of fortress - a defensible homestead for its pioneer owner, August Leue, who arrived in East Africa in 1885 as part of a German military expedition to East Africa. Ngare Sero is the house Leue built when he returned to Africa in retirement to try his hand at coffee and rubber farming on the fertile lower slopes of Mount Meru. Leue was the leader of a group of pioneer German farmers who settled in the region, and his house, then known as 'Leuedorf', was the centre of their community, containing a chapel and a post office, surrounded by high walls and a guard tower behind which the settlers could retreat if danger threatened.

Ngare Sero, as the farmhouse is known today, is Maasai for 'dappled water'. The water in question is a series of mountain springs, flowing together to form sunlight-speckled pools before gushing downwards through the wooded riverbed towards a turbine first installed in 1928. The same system of hydro-electric power is still used to provide some of the electricity for the farmhouse, now converted into a magnificent colonial-style lodge.

The river's pools are surrounded by twenty acres of lush green olive forest, home to troops of Colobus and Sykes monkeys, hooting and crashing in the trees above the stillness of the water. Russet and green pondweed lies on the surface, turned to gold at the beginning and end of the day by the glow of the sun. Dragonflies skip over the surface of the water and waterbirds - the lodge boasts over 200 species of bird just in the immediate vicinity - contemplate the glassy surface while perched statue-still on half-submerged logs.

Ngare Sero still retains many of the original features built by its first owner. Long, colonial verandahs stretch along the front of the house. Long-armed planters' chairs provide a perfect spot from which to contemplate the awesome view of Mount Kilimanjaro as it appears from between the clouds each evening, glaciers burning blood-red then icy blue as the sun sinks lower. Outside, the landscaped grounds, containing just eight rooms, fall in terraces down to the trout pools and riverbed. An Italian sunken garden, complete with marble swimming pool, is alive with the pinks, reds and blues of bougainvillea and jacaranda. When darkness falls, the shrieking croaks of a thousand tree frogs rises to a crescendo, mingling with the soft rushing of water flowing over the volcanic rocks of the riverbed.

Downstairs, the living area has been furnished with low stone benches, topped with brown leather and cream cushions. A substantial fire burns in the stone fireplace, below a mantelpiece filled with antiques commemorating Tanzania's German colonial past - a bust of General Hindenburg sits alongside a stunning Art Deco water flask rescued from the former German State House in Dar es Salaam. Genuine Afghan rugs temper the cold stone of the floor - the nights can be chilly at 1,200m altitude. Upstairs, the two guest suites have a comfortable farmhouse feel, with uneven wooden floorboards creaking underfoot, warm, earthy reds and yellows on the walls, and vast brown Chesterfield sofas scattered with sari silk cushions.

Left: A giant cast-iron chandelier reflects light from the polished wooden pillars in the entrance hall of Ngare Sero Mountain Lodge.

Left and above: The interior spaces of Ngare Sero Mountain Lodge feature rich red walls and heavy dark wood furniture. Golden goblets add a medieval feel to the dining room.

Left: Sari silk cushions are scattered on an Afghan rug at the river's edge - perfect for watching the waterbirds come in to roost as the sun sets.
Above: The carefully landscaped gardens at Ngare Sero are a riot of colour.

Safari Spa

Polo in the shadow of Kilimanjaro

The sight of a dozen sleekly polished thoroughbreds at full gallop in pursuit of a polo ball is a spectacular one at any time. But add to this rush of colour and adrenaline the towering faces of Mount Meru and Mount Kilimanjaro, and the polo field at Safari Spa could well be the most dramatic in the world. For East Africa's two most impressive peaks are spectators at the regular matches that are played on the impeccable green turf of the hotel's own Nduruma Polo Club.

The club comprises an old fashioned stableyard with whitewashed looseboxes lined up around a palm-topped drinking fountain under *makuti* thatch. The tackroom, full of the smell of new hay and oiled leather, is heated by a cast iron stove on colder mornings, and also doubles as a bar during the club's weekly fixtures. The sounds of the stables punctuate each day at Safari Spa - the clop of hooves as the horses pass on morning exercise accompanies breakfast, and a shrill neigh or two sometimes interrupts the silence of the velvety highland night. An elegant carriage, drawn by a handsome bay, is available to take guests on a trip around the surrounding farmland, the centre of a thriving rose growing business that daily sends lorries full of blooms out on their way to the romantics of distant Europe.

Safari Spa is owned and run by Jerome and Zsuzsa Bruins, a Dutch/Hungarian couple who occupy the main farmhouse, a plantation bungalow now converted into a stunning two-storey home. The central space downstairs reflects the family's love of polo, horses and dogs with a series of paintings, photographs and plaster sculptures. Polo mallets are hung on the banisters of the sweeping staircase, with a row of well-worn leather boots, silver trophies and racks of saddles adding to the equestrian feel. In one corner, startlingly large fibreglass marlin heads mounted on wall plaques commemorate record sport fishing catches at the coast. The coast of Tanzania is also reflected in the opposite corner, a pretty space reflecting the colours and textures of Zanzibar - a carved rosewood bench draped with silken Indian fabrics and cushions upholstered in gold and sequins. Family portraits stand in carved frames on top of piles of antique suitcases and trunks, discovered in the markets of Arusha or Tanga. A handsome glass-topped coffee table is filled with more souvenirs of Tanzania's colonial past - old German banknotes, a leather saddle flask, shells, fob watches and playing cards.

The Spa of the hotel's title is a cool green and white space built onto the side of the mess area. The sunlight filters in through emerald ferns and creepers planted along the glass walls that surround a magnificent marble jacuzzi. Alongside is a wood-lined sauna and steam room and a series of treatment rooms for some serious pre or post-safari pampering, followed perhaps by a swim among the palms and bougainvillea of the gardens.

Left: The spectacular jacuzzi pool at Safari Spa, perfect for a relaxing soak after the rigours of a safari.

Left: Marlin heads on the wall commemorate record fishing catches on the coast.
Above: Polo mallets hang from the staircase and saddles line the walls - evidence of the sporting passions of the horse-loving Bruins family.

Above and right: Safari Spa features fascinating antique objects - luggage, hats, binoculars, fans and cameras - mostly collected by the family from markets around East Africa.

Left: The smell of leather and saddle soap permeates the old-fashioned tackroom.
Above: The various horse-drawn vehicles at Safari Spa are still used regularly for travel around the farm.

Left and above: A row of sleek thoroughbred heads look expectantly over the doors of the elegant whitewashed stableyard, prior to an afternoon's thundering action on the polo field.

Justin and Gillian Bell

When Wilderness Africa safari guide Justin Bell decided to build a permanent home at Kiranyi in Arusha, he had only one reason - he needed a place to keep his book collection. Home comforts came a definite second to storage space, so he erected a clapboard house knocked together from offcuts of wood and standing on stilts - thus handily providing a garage for his motorbike at the same time. Facilities were basic - a long-drop loo and outdoor shower at the bottom of the garden - but the new one-room house had bookshelves lining every wall.

As Justin's career as a safari guide took off, however, he found himself away for long periods of time while his home was being constructed. The house was thus built largely as a series of surprises, with Justin leaving instructions for the building crew before taking off into the bush and then returning weeks later to find out how they'd been interpreted. As for guests, the stream of visitors who arrived in those early bachelor days were simply invited to pitch their tents in the garden.

So far so good - Justin had a hilltop eyrie, basic but functional, in which to relax - and of course read - in between his safaris. But things had to change when his future wife Gillian joined him from Zanzibar where she'd been living. The couple's son Laurence was on the way, and Gillian put her foot down when it came to a bathroom at the bottom of the garden, reached only by a ladder and devoid of electricity or hot water! So began the slow transformation of the house from a bachelor bookshelf to a family home.

Over the years, stone walls were erected between the stilts to create a ground floor, extensions added, trees planted, pipes plumbed, and solar electricity installed. By the time the Bell's daughter Alana arrived, the property had been miraculously transformed into a spacious cottage, with a low-ceilinged stone living room where once the motorbike had resided, and a guest bedroom with ensuite bathroom.

The bookshelves, however, stayed, and now line the walls of a sunny bedroom with a verandah that looks out towards the sunset. Despite these new touches of civilisation, though, the progress wasn't all smooth - Gillian still tells the story of a dinner party at which the couple's guests, gathered for genteel drinks on the upstairs balcony, were assailed by clouds of choking, acrid smoke from the huge chunks of pork Justin was attempting to cook on the open fire downstairs.

These days, however, a roomy, tiled kitchen has replaced the open fireplace, and meals are served on the scrubbed wooden worktop or sitting around the circular dining table at one end of the sitting room - a relaxed space of squashy sofas, ethnic cushions and tasselled Indian lampshades. The sitting room is flanked by a playroom, filled with crayon drawings and dressing up costumes by its three- and six year-old proprietors, who scribble happily in between forays in the garden to climb in and out of their wooden treehouse or romp with the latest litter of puppies.

Left: A mangrove wood sofa sits next to the huge stone fireplace in Gillian and Justin's sitting room.

Left and above: The house has been adapted over the years to meet the needs of the Bells' young children, Laurence (above) and Alana (left).

Left: Guests now no longer have to camp in the garden, but are accommodated in the sunny spare room with its cast iron bed and rich, warm fabrics.
Above: Bookshelves still dominate the upstairs bedroom!

Left and above: The house was originally constructed from wooden offcuts and raised on stilts to allow Justin to park his motorbike underneath. The bottom storey has now been filled in, but the upstairs verandah remains the perfect place to watch the sunset.

Aziz and Alice Hajee

Aziz and Alice Hajee's elegant plantation-style mansion is perched on top of a hill in Sangananu Village, just outside Arusha. The whitewashed walls of the house stand out brightly above sweeping, manicured green lawns, with both ghostly white Mount Kilimanjaro and the blue-grey, towering bulk of Mount Meru rising through the clouds at either end of the building.

The house belonged originally to the coffee estate that surrounds it, home of an English banker and sometime farmer who left the business in 1975. From then until 1999, when Aziz Hajee discovered it, the house fell slowly into disrepair, occupied initially by a Polish hunter in between safaris, then later by a collection of cows and goats quartered in the dining room!

Originally from Kenya, Aziz moved to Tanzania to begin his safari guiding business, Tandala Safaris, which takes safari aficionados and even the odd movie star on luxurious holidays around the northern game parks of Tanzania. He was initially drawn to the house because of the mountain views: "I'd always dreamed of seeing a mountain from my bedroom!" he says. Seeing potential even through the house's disrepair, he embarked on an intensive programme of refurbishment, including installing electrical and plumbing systems. The basic structure of the house, however, was intact - a tribute to the German architect who put the building in place back in 1937. Aziz met his French wife, Alice, when she arrived in Arusha to work as a lawyer at the United Nations Tribunal on Rwanda, and she joined him in putting the finishing touches to her new home.

Despite the building's manorial exterior, with its whitewashed walls, leaded windows and wide, sweeping verandahs, the interior design is anything but formal or colonial. Instead it's a relaxed, contemporary space with cool creams and whites predominating. A monumental, textured coffee table and chairs - made from ancient pitted wood salvaged from sunken dhows on the Swahili coast - are surrounded by more modern beige and cream floor cushions and positioned in front of a vast brick fireplace for the chilly cold-season evenings.

The house's décor owes a lot to the textures and colours of natural objects - skulls, bones, fossils, skins and feathers are to be found everywhere, lined up along the walls of the verandah or filling corners inside the long, open plan dining/sitting room. All of these have been collected by Aziz on his safaris in Kenya and Tanzania, journeys which are also the source of the framed wildlife photographs on the walls of the study and hallway.

Upstairs, the master bedroom opens onto a wide, curved balcony, in which the glittering peak of Kilimanjaro appears framed above the railings, an apparition that can be enjoyed from the vast wooden double bed inside, a modern piece of furniture simply draped in white chiffon covers. Reclining chairs and potted plants make this upstairs balcony the perfect place for a leisurely breakfast, enjoying the view and the cool morning air that rises from the lush green gardens below.

Left: Rugged, pitted wood salvaged from a sunken dhow was used to create this coffee table, surrounded by ethnic cushions and filled with skins, shells and teeth collected on Aziz's safaris.

Above and right: The interior of Aziz and Alice's house is filled with dozens of organic objects such as fossils, skulls, seed pods and porcupine quills, alongside ethnic artefacts collected from Africa and Asia.

Left and above: The upstairs and downstairs verandahs are relaxed spaces, with wooden furniture draped in natural fabrics.

George and Deborah Mavroudis

George Mavroudis - professional safari guide, naturalist and photographer - is a third-generation Tanzanian of Greek Cypriot extraction, born and bred in Dar es Salaam. After an education in Europe, he returned to Tanzania to work as a wildlife research assistant, then a safari guide. He met his Boston-born wife Deborah while they were both working at Abercrombie and Kent, and in 1992 the couple set up their own safari company, a small, personal operation guiding private clients around remote wildlife and culture areas in East Africa.

George and Deborah's safari clients are often invited to the couple's magnificent home in Momella, outside Arusha, for tea or dinner after a long journey through the bush. The house, now almost ten years old, was built from scratch, with local architects and designers creating both the house and garden. The lack of ready materials meant that experimentation and local expertise and innovation were needed to bring the house into being. The warm, glowing earthenware tiles that line the entrance hall and veranda, for instance, were commissioned from a local potter, the first job of this kind he'd ever done. The heavy, gothic-style cast iron lanterns which hang dramatically throughout the house were designed by Deborah herself and created by students at Arusha Technical College.

The house itself is a modern take on an old-fashioned Tanzanian planter's house, looking down across rolling lawns and flowerbeds filled with rambling roses to the distant hills of Maasailand. The old fashioned leaded windows of the traditional plantation building have been reinvented as a contemporary wall of French panes, surrounded by black metal frames. The windows reach almost floor to ceiling, giving the atrium a unique texture as well as an overwhelming sense of light and space, with the colours of the garden and the sky beyond entering the interior through the modern, symmetrical pattern of the window panes.

On either side of the house, a second storey has recently been built under the eaves, to provide extra space for the three Mavroudis children - Taylor, 5, Benjamin, 7, and Damon, 9. Downstairs, the split-level living and dining room is connected by a gigantic, two-sided brick stove, one fireplace facing towards each half of the room. The fireplace hood, a magnificent bronzed piece of metal, is another local invention borne of necessity - with no real bronze or brass available, ordinary metal was painted with linseed oil to give it a coppery sheen.

The overall interior design of the house has a distinctly Byzantine, medieval-religious feel to it - icons, designed and made by George's mother, hang on the walls and form a magnificent frieze above the dining table, based on a 13th century Greek mural. Gothic, upright chairs surround the table, which is adorned with heavy silver chalices and candlesticks inlaid with glowing polished stone, and a turquoise Moroccan enamel dish. Gold brocade sofas and thronelike chairs are covered with vibrant velvet tasselled cushions, bringing a warmth and grandeur to the cool and contemporary feel of the architect's original design.

Left: The Mavroudis' magnificent dining table, backed by a frieze depicting a thirteenth-century Greek mural.

Above: The sunny verandah, hung with metal lanterns and lookng out across Maasailand.

Right: The vast earthenware fireplace with its bronzed metal hood is surrounded by tapestry fabrics and heavy wooden tables topped with coloured ceramics and beaten silver candlesticks.

Left and above: The entrance hall, with its polished sideboard and giant mirror, is flooded with light from the floor-to-ceiling windows that lead out into the garden.

Roland and Zoe Purcell

Roland and Zoe Purcell's home is more of an encampment - or perhaps a fortress - than a single house, comprising a small village of wooden offices, stone towers, and a series of lean-tos and sheds grouped together on a hilltop at Usa River, near Arusha. The nerve centre of the whole operation - Zoe and Roland run Greystoke Safaris, the company behind two of Tanzania's most original and remote camps - is their castle-cottage, a fantastical, near-circular stone building, with pointed, gothic windows, wooden shutters, and a courtyard that looks as though it should be entered through a portcullis. Exterior stairs run up to the battlements on the second floor, where tiny doors provide peepholes from which to spy out visitors as they approach up the hill.

The house was originally conceived as an office, but Roland and Zoe found that they were spending more and more time in this spot on their site, enjoying the sense of space and freedom that comes from the near 360° view of surrounding Maasailand. So they shelved plans to build their own dwelling further down the hill, and instead left their wooded river valley as a wild space inhabited by bushbuck, Sykes and vervet monkeys, owls and bushbabies.

Inside, the central sitting room takes up the whole height of the house, with the upper storeys reached by sharply sloping wooden ladders forming a pyramid on either side of the front door. Above the entrance hangs a gigantic black-and-white portrait of a grizzled male chimpanzee. This is Bembe, now sadly deceased, one of the inhabitants of the remote Mahale Mountains National Park, site of the Purcell's innovative Greystoke Camp. Messages from both Greystoke and the company's other camp, Chada - located in the Katavi National Park in the far west of Tanzania - are relayed via a long-range radio that sits in the warm farmhouse-style kitchen, innocuous among the hanging copper pots and pans, strings of dried chillis and scrubbed wooden work surfaces.

Silken Arthurian pennants - the Purcells have a fancy for the medieval and the gothic - hang from the balconies down into the room, one corner of which is occupied by a huge brick fireplace and a pair of faded sofas draped with rugs and skins. On the carved mantelpiece, once the post of a Swahili door, sits a collection of objects ranging from the kitsch (a mannequin's head adorned with a handlebar moustache and a Russian hat) to the macabre (a snake embalmed in a bottle of vodka).

Upstairs, galvanised ladders lead up to the top of the building, a space shared by the two Purcell children in tiny bedrooms - one pink, one yellow - tucked under the eaves on either side of a rich red-painted Victorian bathroom, the claw bath standing under a window looking down two floors into the sitting room below. Underneath is a sumptuous fin-de-siecle walk-in wardrobe, scattered with silks, shoes and tiaras, strictly a 'girls only' domain for Zoe and her daughter Isabella, and perfect for dressing up before one of the family's famously wild parties.

Left: Roland and Zoe's kitchen, complete with gothic windows and long-range radio.

Above: An attic bedroom is painted bright pink for the Purcell's daughter, Isabella.
Right: The Victorian-style bathroom is perched high in the rafters, with a window next to the bath for keeping an eye on things downstairs while performing one's ablutions!

Above: Shelves are set under the ladder-like stairs in a clever use of space.
Right: The Purcells' magnificent high-ceilinged sitting room, hung with Arthurian pennants and dominated by a giant chimpanzee portrait.

The 'exotic wilderness' of Africa has captured the imagination of moviemakers and moviegoers as long as celluloid has existed. In Hollywood's golden era, legions of glamorous stars were transported by armies of retainers deep into the bush, to smoulder and pout against the flame of the sunset or fall helplessly into each other's arms as herds of buffalo charged past across the plains. The audiences loved it.

Tanzania has hosted its fair share of Hollywood film crews, whose safaris rivalled that of the most demanding hunters in their size and complexity. The safari for the 1950 film version of H Rider Haggard's *King Solomon's Mines*, starring Deborah Kerr and Stewart Granger, was described by one American newspaper as 'the most ambitious location trip in Hollywood history', involving a 14,000 mile round trip accompanied by 53 European filmmakers and over 130 Africans. The stunts on King Solomon's Mines included a co-ordinated stampede of 6,000 animals on the Serengeti plains.

The filming of *Mogambo*, a romantic adventure starring Clark Gable, Grace Kelly and Ava Gardner, was described by its safari outfitter Bunny Allen as 'like running a small war'. Frank Sinatra turned up on the set to keep an eye on his fiancée Gardner and her co-star Gable, and found time to serenade the assembled crew with a rendition of 'White Christmas' in camp on Christmas Eve.

Grizzled Western star John Wayne was at home on the African range in the 1962 film *Hatari*, an action comedy involving a motley group of European characters who converge in Momella, in the shadow of Mount Meru, to capture animals alive for zoos in America. One of the film's stars, blonde German actor Hardy Kruger, enjoyed his experience so much he bought the farmhouse used in the film set for himself and eschewed Hollywood briefly for a life of hunting and farming around present-day Arusha National Park.

Left above: Ava Gardner and Clark Gable in *Mogambo*.
below: A location scene from the 1950 movie *King Solomon's Mines*.
Right: Elsa Martinelli, surprised in her bath, in *Hatari*.

Contact Addresses

Chada Camp
Greystoke Safaris
PO Box 681, Usa River, Tanzania
Tel: +255 27 255 3820/3821
Email: info@mahale.co.tz
www.mahale.co.tz

Greystoke Camp
Greystoke Safaris
PO Box 681, Usa River, Tanzania
Tel: +255 27 255 3820/3821
Email: info@mahale.co.tz
www.mahale.co.tz

Grumeti River Camp
Conservation Corporation Africa
P/Bag X27, Benmore, 2010, Johannesburg
Block F, Pinmill Farm, Katherine
St, Sandton, South Africa
Tel: +27 11 809 4300
Fax: +27 11 809 4400
Email: webenquiries@ccafrica.com
www.ccafrica.com

Kikoti Camp
PO Box 284, Arusha, Tanzania
Tel: +255 27 2508790
Fax: +255 27 2508896
Email: tzphotosafaris@habari.co.tz
www.tzphotosafaris.com

Kirawira Luxury Tented Camp
Serena Hotels Ltd
6th Floor, AICC, Ngorongoro Wing
PO Box 2551, Arusha, Tanzania
Tel: +255 27 2506304
Fax: +255 27 2504155
Email: reservations@serena.co.tz
www.serenahotels.com

Klein's Camp
Conservation Corporation Africa
P/Bag X27, Benmore, 2010, Johannesburg
Block F, Pinmill Farm, Katherine
St, Sandton, South Africa
Tel: +27 11 809 4300
Fax:+27 11 809 4400
Email: webenquiries@ccafrica.com
www.ccafrica.com

Kusini Camp
Sanctuary Lodges
PO Box 427
Arusha, Tanzania
Tel: +255 27 250 8346
Fax +255 27 250 8273
Email: tanzania@sanctuarylodges.com
www.sanctuarylodges.com

Lake Manyara Tree Lodge
Conservation Corporation Africa
P/Bag X27, Benmore, 2010, Johannesburg
Block F, Pinmill Farm, Katherine
St, Sandton, South Africa
Tel: +27 11 809 4300
Fax: +27 11 809 4400
Email: webenquiries@ccafrica.com
www.ccafrica.com

Migration Camp
Halcyon Tanzania Ltd
PO Box 1861, Arusha, Tanzania
Tel/fax: +255 27 250 9277-81
Email: res@halcyontz.com
www.halcyontz.com

Mwagusi Safari Camp
Tropic Africa
14 Castelnau, London SW13 9RU, UK
Tel/fax: +44 208 846 9363
Email: tropicafrica.uk@virgin.net
www.ruaha.org

Ngare Sero Mountain Lodge
PO Box 425, Arusha, Tanzania
Tel: +255 27 255 3638
Email: ngare-sero-lodge@habari.co.tz

Ngorongoro Crater Lodge
Conservation Corporation Africa
P/Bag X27, Benmore, 2010, Johannesburg
Block F, Pinmill Farm, Katherine
St, Sandton, South Africa
Tel: +27 11 809 4300
Fax: +27 11 809 4400
Email: webenquiries@ccafrica.com
www.ccafrica.com

Oliver's Camp
PO Box 425, Arusha, Tanzania
Tel/fax: +255 27 2508548
Email: olivers@habari.co.tz
www.oliverscamp.com

Ruaha River Lodge
Foxtreks Ltd
PO Box 10270, Dar es Salaam, Tanzania
Tel: +255 741 237422
Fax: +255 741 327706
Email: fox@twiga.com
www.ruahariverlodge.com

Safari Spa
PO Box 988 Arusha , Tanzania
Tel: +255 27 2553264
Email: safarispa@habari.co.tz

Sand Rivers Selous
PO Box 1344, Dar es Salaam, Tanzania
Tel: +255 741 768153
Fax: +255 22 2865156
Email:sand-rivers@intafrica.com
www.sandrivers.com

Selous Safari Camp
Box 1192 Dar es Salaam, Tanzania
Tel: +255 22 2134794
Fax: +255 22 2112794
Email:info@selous.com
www.selous.com

Sokwe
PO Box 3052, Arusha, Tanzania
Tel: +255 27 2548182
Fax: +255 27 2548320
Email: enquiries@sokwe.com
www.sokwe.com

Swala Camp
Sanctuary Lodges
PO Box 427
Arusha, Tanzania
Tel: +255 27 250 8346
Fax +255 27 250 8273
Email: tanzania@sanctuarylodges.com
www.sanctuarylodges.com

Tarangire Treetops
Halcyon Tanzania Ltd
PO Box 1861, Arusha, Tanzania
Tel/fax: +255 27 250 9277-81
Email: res@halcyontz.com
www.halcyontz.com

The following airlines provide internal flights within Tanzania:

Coastal Aviation
PO Box 3052
107 Upanga Road
Dar es Salaam, Tanzania
Tel: +255 22 2117959
Fax: +255 22 2118647
Email: safari@coastal.cc
www.coastal.cc

Precision Air
PO Box 1636
Arusha, Tanzania
Tel: +255 27 2506903
Fax: +255 27 2508204
Email:
information@precisionairtz.com
www.precisionairtz.com

Regional Air
PO Box 14755
Arusha, Tanzania
Tel: +255 27 2502541
Fax: +255 27 2544164
Email: info@regional.co.tz
www.airkenya.com

Acknowledgments

The authors would like to extend heartfelt thanks to the following people for invaluable assistance during the course of the Safari Living project:
Hon Zakia Meghji, Minister for Tourism and Natural Resources, Director General Mr Bigurube and Public Relations Manager Mr James Lembeli of Tanzania National Parks, Mr Emmanuel Chausi of Ngorongoro Crater Conservation Area, Benson Kibonde of Selous Game Reserve, Caroline Blummer at Regional Air, Rashida Patwa and Anna Westh at Coastal Aviation, Gulf Air in London, David Sem at Precision Air, Shayne Richardson and Martine Karpes of CC Africa, Roland and Zoe Purcell of Greystoke Safaris, Dean Yeadon of Halcyon Ltd, Chris Fox of Mwagusi Safari Camp, Charles Dobie of Selous Safari Company, Marlise Alpers of Sanctuary Lodges, Derik le Grange and Lilane van Der Merwe of Serena Active, Salim Janmohamed and Shafina Mohamed of Serena Hotels, Pratik and Sonia Patel of Tanzania Photographic Safaris, Nuru and Khairoon Jafferji in Dar es Salaam, Zulfiqar Khanbhai, Abdul and Salma Khanbhai, Hatim and Rashida Khanbhai and Justin and Gillian Bell in Arusha.

At the camps, the authors are indebted to the following people for making each photoshoot possible:
Rawanna and Murray at Chada Camp, Tonya and Pete at Crater Lodge, Jimmy and Daniela at Greystoke Camp, Peter at Grumeti River Lodge, Neil at Jongomero, Hilda at Kikoti Camp, Charles at Kirawira, Faustini at Klein's Camp, Colin and Karen at Kusini Camp, Francis and Naringo at Lake Manyara Tree Lodge, Patrick at Migration Camp, Helle at Mwagusi Camp, Mike, Tim, Stasia and Gisella at Ngare Sero Mountain Lodge, Paul and Tati at Oliver's Camp, Peter and Sarah at Ruaha River Lodge, Zsusza and Jerome at Safari Spa, Alex and team at Sand Rivers Selous, Sal, Vonan and Nicky at Selous Safari Camp, Glen and Cindy at Swala Camp, and Alfred at Tarangire Treetops.

Many thanks to the following people for allowing us to photograph their homes:
Justin and Gillian Bell, Aziz and Alice Hajee, George and Deborah Mavroudis, and Roland and Zoe Purcell.

Thanks also to Mervin Ng in Singapore, to Sean Qureshi of Spectrum Colour Lab in Nairobi,
Zarina Jafferji for her help on our Tarangire photoshoot, to Shabani our tireless driver, to Terence, Antony and Ali here at Zanzibar Gallery Publishers, and to Abid and Bashira Jafferji for all their help and support. Special thanks also to Nigel and Lois Pitcher for their eagle-eyed proof reading!
Finally, many thanks to my dearest wife Kulsum for her patience during my long absences on safari.

The writer is indebted to the authors of the following books for reference material used in the text:
Bartle Bull - *Safari*. Penguin, London, 1988
Kenneth M Cameron - *Into Africa*. Constable, London, 1990

Photo credits - many thanks to the following for permission to reproduce photographs:
Page 151: Ulf Aschan
Page 219: Alfred Leo, Lions Safari International
Text credit:
Page 91: Geoffrey Weill, CC Africa

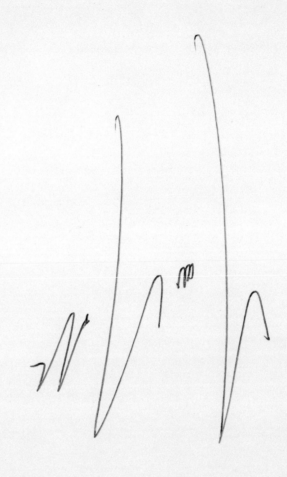